Best Friends,
Occasional Enemies

Best Friends, Occasional Enemies

The Lighter Side of Life as a Mother and Daughter

Lisa Scottoline

AND

Francesca Serritella

ST. MARTIN'S PRESS ⋈ NEW YORK

www.stmartins.com

All photographs courtesy of the authors except where noted.

Library of Congress Cataloging-in-Publication Data

Scottoline, Lisa.
    Best friends, occasional enemies : the lighter side of life as a mother and daughter / Lisa Scottoline and Francesca Serritella. — 1st ed.
        p. cm.
    ISBN 978-0-312-65163-3
    1. Mothers and daughters—Humor. 2. Women—Humor.
3. Scottoline, Lisa. 4. Serritella, Francesca Scottoline.
I. Serritella, Francesca Scottoline. II. Title.
    PN6231.M68S37 2011
    818'.5402—dc23

                                                    2011025863

First Edition: November 2011

10 9 8 7 6 5 4 3 2 1

To mothers and daughters everywhere, with love

Contents

|||||||||||||||||||||||||||||||||||||||||||||||||||

Best Friends,

Occasional Enemies

Introduction

|||||||||||||||||||||||||||||||||||||||||||||||||

By Lisa

Here's what I've learned in my life: Motherhood has no expiration date.

This means that even though Daughter Francesca has grown up and moved out of the house, I'm still busy being her mother.

And, happily, her best friend.

We talk on the phone a few times a day, usually while she's walking her dog or I'm walking mine. Our dogs know all our secrets.

Read this, and so will you.

But to stay on point, even though my mother, Mother Mary, is eighty-six years old, and I'm fifty-five, she's still busy being *my* mother. We talk on the phone, too, but less often, because her voice is always in my head. It warns me not to buy dented cans, not to leave my blowdryer near the sink, and not to put too much spaghetti on my fork or I'll choke. Her message is always the same—beware, watch out, and small electrical appliances can be lethal.

But her voice has protected me since the day it took up residence in my head, unpacking its suitcase and its traveling backscratcher. Later, when I got to be a mother myself, I became Mother Mary, only with a better car.

It's inevitable, no?

And now my voice will probably always be in Francesca's head.

Poor thing.

Raising her, I came to understand, with a sort of suburban awe, the uniqueness, the strength, and the power of the bond between mother and daughter. Mother love is like no other, and that's why we love our mothers so deeply, and also why we want to throw them out the window.

Just kidding.

But that's the point.

This is a book about the true-life laughter in the relationship between mother and daughter, written by Daughter Francesca and me. Open it and laugh along. You'll read about a power outage that empowers us, toenail clippings that make us look at each other funny, and a green jacket that becomes a battleground.

I bet you can relate, whether you have a daughter or not. After all, every woman is a daughter. And daughterhood doesn't have an expiration date, either.

Also included herein are stories about life as a woman, at any age. Ladies of a certain age, like me, will recognize yourselves in my stories because we all struggle with the same things, like duvet covers, the preemptive pee, and aging gracefully, which is overrated.

I'm just like every other middle-aged woman, except that I'm divorced twice (from Thing One and Thing Two) and I kiss my dogs on the lips.

These things are not related.

I hope.

My cats won't let me kiss them, as they don't care who pays the mortgage.

Those of you who are younger will see yourselves in Francesca's quest for romance, as well as her struggles with her new apartment, which came with mice (free of charge), plus one creepy exterminator. Francesca's moved to the city, making a life on her own.

With Mom on speed dial.

Finally, every woman will find her mother in our Mother Mary. For example, if your mother has ever said to you, "Don't use that tone with me," you'll know what I mean.

If your daughter has said it to you, too, welcome to the club.

So read on, to stories of our life. We tell the truth about each other, as well as Mother Mary. Three generations of women, sometimes under the same roof. It's either a lovefest, or atomic war.

Enjoy!

And *ka-boom*!

The Occasional Enemies Part

||||||||||||||||||||||||||||||||||||||||||||||||||||

By Lisa

Daughter Francesca and I are very close, but that doesn't mean we don't fight.

On the contrary, it means we do.

So if you're currently fighting with your daughter, or merely fussing from time to time, you've come to the right place.

Let's start with the notion that the no-fighting model isn't the best for mother-daughter relations. I know so many women who feel bad, guilty, or inferior because they fight with their daughters, and they needn't. To them, and to you, I say, flip it.

What?

Flip that notion on its head. If you fight with your daughter, you raised her to think independently from you, and to voice her own views.

Yay!

You're a great mother. Know why?

Because the world doesn't reward the timid. Especially if they have ovaries.

In my opinion, conflict between mother and daughter is normal and good. Not only that, it's love. I say this not as a social scientist, which I'm not, but as a real-life mother, which

I so am. So if your daughter is fighting with you, here's the good and bad news:

The good news is you raised her right.

The bad is you have a headache.

Forever.

Just kidding.

Francesca and I are best friends, but at times, we're at odds. Enemies, only momentarily. Like most mothers and daughters, we're so attuned to each other's words and gestures that even the arching of an eyebrow can convey deep meaning.

If somebody plucks, we're in trouble.

We never have really huge fights, but we have car rides to New York that can feel as if they last cross-country.

Wars of words.

We go on and on, each replying to the other, swept along in a girl vortex of words, during which we parse every nuance of every syllable, with special attention to tone.

Tone is the kryptonite of mother-daughter relationships.

As in, "I don't like your tone."

Also, "Don't use that tone with me."

And the ever-popular, "It wasn't what you said, it was your tone."

It was ever thus. Francesca and I got along great from the time she came out of the egg, and I used to tell her that she wasn't allowed to whine, but she could argue with me. In other words, make her case for whatever she wanted.

Never mind that she was three at the time.

Oddly, this turned out great. She was the Perry Mason of toddlers, and more often than not, she was right. Or she felt completely heard, which was often enough for kiddie satisfaction.

She argued for punch balls from the gift shop at the zoo, dessert before dinner if she ate all her dinner, and the wearing of Cinderella outfits on an almost daily basis, complete with tiara.

What girl doesn't want a tiara?

Another thing I did when she was little was to let her vent. I had no idea how I came upon this idea, but I used to give her the chance to say anything she wanted to me, without interruption, for a full minute.

And I mean, *anything*.

She was even permitted to curse at me, though she didn't know any profanity at that age. It got only as rude as "butt face."

Ouch?

She's still permitted to argue with me and vent her anger. And she accords me the same permission. Even though we're writing books together and we adore each other, we can still get mad at each other. And that valve releases the pressure from the combustible engine that is the mother-daughter relationship.

It's just hot air, anyway.

Bottom line, we're close, so we fight, and the converse is also true. The conflict strengthens us, because it's honesty, hard-earned.

And the more honest we are with each other, the closer we are. You'll see exactly what I mean, in the pages that follow.

So enjoy.

And watch your tone.

We Are All Ferraris

By Lisa

I just got home from a terrible blind date, and that's the good news.

Because it was still a date, so it counts.

It got me out of the house on a Saturday night, all eyelined and underwired, and though it ended badly, I still regard it as a good thing.

Why?

Well, it's not that I feel the need to go out, though I never do.

And it's not that I feel the need to have dates, though I've had only a handful in the past four years, most of them blind.

Not literally, which would probably help.

Bottom line, if I remembered sex, I'd miss it.

But I'm not all pathetic and sad about it, and if you find yourself in a similar position, you shouldn't feel bad, either.

Here's why.

You're not alone. You may feel that way, thanks to TV commercials for breath mints and Valentine's Day, but you're not the only one.

There's me.

And there's lots of women like us, who end up manless in middle age, whether by choice or not. I know, because I get lots of heartfelt emails from widows and divorcées, as I am becoming the poster child for inadvertent celibacy. By which I mean, not woe-is-me celibacy, but more like, Oh, has it really been that long?

Also, why don't I miss it, when I used to like it well enough?

And why aren't I on a mission to find a man?

To begin, let me tell you about my blind date. I thought he was nice, handsome, and smart, which is three more things than I ever expect. And we were having a great time, yapping away through his first and second vodka. But by the time he got to his third vodka, his words slurred, his eyes glistened, and he blurted out the following:

"I miss my girlfriend. I don't know why she broke up with me. The kids didn't like her, but I did."

Uh oh.

This would not be a happy ending. He told me the next day that it was the only time he'd ever tried to kiss somebody who was putting her car into reverse.

That would be me, and can you even believe he went in for the good-night smooch?

Could it be worse?

No.

But even that isn't the point.

Don't miss out on the fullness of your life because something is missing. Take a lesson from my horrible blind date. He was bemoaning the loss of his girlfriend, when he had a perfectly fine woman sitting across from him, ready, willing, and able.

Oh, so able.

In other words, a man is not a passport to life. If you're alone, you can't go into suspended animation. You have to live your life and you can be happy.

You just have to make yourself happy.

How?

Flip it. If you think that being on your own is the problem, turn that idea on its head. Make being alone a bonus. If you're on your own, you don't have to ask anybody's permission to do anything, or take anyone else's opinion into account.

You're not single, you're *a capella*!

And all you need to do is figure out what makes you happy.

So try things. Try anything. Paint. Draw. Take piano lessons. Read a book. Keep a journal. Write a story. Go to night school. Volunteer. Sing. Rearrange the furniture. Join something.

Dance!

Do whatever you like. And since I bet you've spent most of your life taking care of others, take care of yourself. Get your hair done. Your nails. Spend a little money on yourself. You deserve it. Buy a new outfit and parade around.

Look at you, girl!

If you're unsure what else to try, here are some of the things that make me happy: namely, my daughter, dogs, friends, work, books, reading, cats, a big TV, a pony, opera, and chocolate cake.

My life and my heart are full, and I don't feel lonely, though I live alone.

As for the occasional date, if it happens, great. But if it doesn't, I'll live.

Happily.

So make yourself happy, and maybe along the way, you'll meet a man who doesn't like vodka so much, but no matter.

The point isn't him.

It's you.

For once.

And, finally.

Sometimes I visualize myself as an exotic sports car, like a Maserati or a Ferrari, that leaves its garage only occasionally.

Not everybody can drive me, and I don't wait to be driven.

I'm not that kind of car.

And neither are you.

So hit the gas, and live.

All's Fair In Love and Wardrobe

By Francesca

My mom is a great dresser. Mostly because she's wearing my clothes.

When I was growing up, this wasn't a problem. She was never the Dina Lohan mom, wearing low-rider jeans and a too-tight Abercrombie & Fitch top. Back then, she had better clothes than I did. It was the 90's; I waffled between wanting to dress like Alicia Silverstone in *Clueless* and Lisa "Left Eye" Lopes from TLC.

Cargo pants, anyone?

As if.

But now that I've grown out of the teeny-bopper phase, my clothes must look more appealing.

My mother has become a cougar for clothes.

Somewhere along the line, I noticed my mom buying duplicates of anything she bought for me. I got new jeans—she bought a second pair in her size. I needed a winter coat—she ordered two of the same from L.L. Bean. She said it was more convenient that way.

I'm not going to be a baby about it. We live in different cities, so it's not like we're going to be seen together wearing the same outfit.

Or so I thought.

For the last book my mom and I wrote together, I went on my first full-fledged promotional tour. We had scheduled television appearances and signings all over the tri-state area. I was nervous about everything, but like any girl, my main concern was what to wear. I worried about this a month in advance, regularly rifling through my closet on the hunt for suitable clothes.

I agonized on the phone to my mother. She asked, "Don't you have a nice jacket, like a blazer or something? You must."

After more than a decade of book tours, my mother's closet is chock-full of fabulous jackets—tweed, herringbone, suede, silk, leather—you name it, she's worn it. It was hard for her to believe I didn't have one, but it was the truth. I've been supporting myself with my writing, and the dress code for a home office isn't exactly corporate-chic. And my trusty job-interview suit looked like it had been through the war.

So the next time I was home, my mom took me to the mall and generously offered to buy me this lovely green jacket—it was soft, well-tailored, classic. Wearing it, I felt that little jolt of confidence I needed for tour. I was pumped.

A week later, my mom and I were talking on the phone again, and she mentioned in passing that she had ordered the jacket for herself in a size up.

"Don't worry, we won't wear them at the same time," she said.

Right.

Right?

So tour rolls around, and I'm packing to leave for Pennsylvania. Of course the green jacket is coming with me, tags still on, pristine in its garment bag, and I also bring a few nice sweaters and a tweed dress. That should cover it.

But, the morning of our very first signing, my mom peeks her head in my bedroom.

"Are you wearing the green jacket?" she asked.

"Well, I—"

"—'Cause I'm thinking I'm gonna wear the green jacket. Unless you want to. But you should wear that dress, the dress looks great on you."

I concede and wear the dress. But despite my early acquiescence, my mother repeats this little routine for the next three days of tour. If I hesitate at all, she's wearing the jacket.

Harrumph.

"Mom," I say, smiling, on the fourth day of this. "Don't you think it's a little funny that with your entire closet full of blazers, the one thing you want to wear is the one item I also own?"

"Don't say, 'it's funny,' when you don't really think it's funny. It's passive-aggressive. If you're annoyed, just say so."

But see, when your mother says, "Just say so," she doesn't mean it. She means, "Don't you dare say so." I knew this, and yet . . .

"Alright, I'm annoyed!"

Petty bickering ensued. And then, the inevitable:

"I have a solution," my mom said. "Why don't we both wear the jacket?"

I gave her some serious "seriously?" eyebrows.

"It'll be cute!"

No. Just no. Mother-daughter matching outfits were barely cute when I was a baby, they certainly aren't cute now.

Somehow, after the fray, neither of us ended up wearing the jacket.

Typical.

But life goes on. We were both having a great time at the signing, and I had nearly forgotten about our wardrobe dysfunction when someone in the audience asked a very nice question:

"You two seem to have the perfect relationship. Do you ever fight?"

My mom shot me a grin. "Should we tell them?"

She recounted (a slightly biased version of) our silly argument and then posed the question, "It'd be cute if we matched, right?"

She honestly thought the crowd was going to side with her.

That's why I love my mother.

Of course, our lovely, intelligent, reasonable audience shouted a chorus of "NO!"

And that's why I love our readers.

Empowered

||||||||||||||||||||||||||||||||||||||||||||||||||

By Lisa

There's nothing like a power outage to bring a family closer.
To killing each other.

Let me explain. Daughter Francesca came home because
we're about to embark on an eight-day trip to Rome, which
is four days of book tour, plus four days of sightseeing. I'm a
lucky author to have a European book tour, and luckier still to
have Francesca come along, not only because she's fun but also
because she speaks Italian.

All I can say in Italian is pasta.

My books are translated into 30 languages, and I speak only
carbohydrates.

To get to the point, we're set to depart on Sunday night, so
I bring Francesca home on Thursday, with dog Pip in tow, and
when we hit the house, we discover that the power is off from
a summer storm.

The good news is that I installed a generator last year, which
means that five things in my house should still be running. I
can't remember which things, so I go around checking. You
know where I go first.

The refrigerator is fine.

So's the water and a TV in the kitchen.

And so's the oven, so you see my priorities immediately.

But no air-conditioning.

Not even a fan.

I know this sounds spoiled, but it's ninety degrees in the family room.

But I'm getting ahead of myself, because at that moment, I'm thinking the outage is temporary and might even be fun. Francesca agrees. So we have a chuckle, go make dinner, and eat. It's our candlelight adventure until the TV stops working, because the cable is down.

Hmmm.

This is usually the time when someone says how great it is when the electricity goes off, and people can really talk to each other, and blah blah blah.

I disagree.

I like electricity.

I'm power-hungry.

Plus the Internet and TV don't prevent me from talking to my daughter. We're a family of two women. We never shut up.

By nightfall, there's still no power. I'm bummed that the sink is full of dirty dishes. She's bummed that its ninety-three degrees in the family room. And upstairs in the bedrooms, it's even hotter.

Long story short, by bedtime, we begin to disagree. Francesca wants to sleep in the family room with the screen door open, but I say no, because psycho killers will enter and do their worst.

We have our first fight of the weekend.

I win, which means we sweat upstairs, safe and sound, but it turns out that she's right, because Little Tony, my black-and-tan

Cavalier King Charles Spaniel, almost has heatstroke. We move downstairs to the family room.

Psycho killers stay away, as they like air-conditioning, too.

Day Two dawns, and we sweat and swelter. We can't do much but eat and we did that already. We're not fighting per se, but we don't like each other's tones. I know that I'm the cranky one. I whine and complain about the heat, the electric company, and the oil spill in the Gulf, for good measure. On the other hand, Francesca keeps coming up with ideas to solve our predicament.

Who raised this child?

Her Day Two idea is that we should go to an air-conditioned place to cool down, so we go to the mall and buy mascara.

This is what girls do in an emergency.

But I find myself cheering up, so we stick with her plan, and on Night Two, we go to the movies and see *Knight and Day*. We become friends again, as we like Tom Cruise. Francesca dubs the power outage Tom Cruise Appreciation Week.

On Day Three, I call the electric company just to yell at the recording, but Francesca's Night Three idea is that we go sit outside in the backyard, where it's cool, and watch a DVD on my laptop, which still has some battery power.

I start whining. "Are you serious? It's dark and there are bugs."

She says, "We can watch *Collateral*. It'll be like a drive-in movie."

"But what about the psycho killers?"

"Mom, it's Tom Cruise Appreciation Week."

And she's right. So we go outside and sit on two beach chairs with five dogs and a laptop. The moon is full, casting bright shadows on the lawn, and the fireflies twinkle around us, like peridots in the air.

Our power struggle is over.

And we sit, happily, in the dark.

Picture Day

|||||||||||||||||||||||||||||||||||||||||||||||||

By Lisa

I read in the paper that nowadays, the companies who take school pictures will retouch the photos to remove the kids' cowlicks, missing front teeth, and freckles.

This is not progress.

Reportedly, ten percent of parents request such retouching. The other ninety percent love their children.

Apparently, some parents like to see their children as they should be, instead of how they are. Or maybe they're Photoshopaholics.

I can't think of a better message a parent can send a child than, "You're almost good enough!"

I never saw a photo of Daughter Francesca that I would retouch. I loved her face and the way it changed as she grew up. Plus the retouching cost seventeen dollars. Parents who request it should put the money toward their child's eventual therapy bill.

This doesn't mean that some kids wouldn't benefit from retouching, or even that some kids aren't downright ugly. Lots of us have faces only a mother would love, especially during our Wonder Years.

Me, especially.

I look back on my school pictures with a queasy feeling, and that's as it should be.

Let me explain.

I was smokin' hot until I turned two years old, then it went from bad to worse, when my baby teeth fell out, only to be replaced by two front teeth that stuck straight out, defying gravity. They used to call them buck teeth, but that would be kind. No buck had these teeth. As a toddler, I could have built a dam.

Also, my nose, which started out cute and little, grew and grew and forgot to stop. It popped out like Pinocchio's, and I'm not lying. The Flying Scottolines have big noses. Mother Mary says that we get more oxygen than anybody else, and she's right. If we breathe in, you're dead.

Plus, my eyes, which looked so round and blue when my nose was little, seemed to shrink and flatten as my nose got bigger, and then I got thick glasses, so I looked like a beaver with corrective lenses.

The proof is my school pictures, which reflect all those hideous stages of my life, all the zits and tinsel teeth and pixie haircuts and horrible clothes. Still, I don't think Mother Mary would have retouched a single picture. She loved me the way I was and she would have spent the seventeen bucks on cigarettes.

Plus, retouching a school photo would have taken all the fun out of Picture Day. Do you remember that excitement? In the Scottoline household, Picture Day was circled on the calendar, and it was a big deal. Brother Frank and I wore our best clothes, and we got combs at school.

Free!

It's always exciting to get something free, even a comb. Now,

Yes, this is the retake.

we watch Oprah, where she gives away her favorite things, for free. Cars, TVs, lasagna pans. You know what my favorite thing would be?

Being Oprah's favorite thing.

But back to Picture Day.

I remember long lines of kids leading to a mysterious black curtain set up in the gym, and when you were finally ushered behind the curtain, you were in the presence of the photographer, as personable as the Wizard of Oz. He would order you to smile, blind you with a flash, and get you out of there, reeling.

Then you would wait and wait until pictures came in, which was another day of excitement. There would be the various photo packages to choose from, and you'd end up with 383,898 wallet-size photos, even if you knew only four wallets.

When those photos came back, if you looked good, you showed everybody. And if you didn't, everybody knew.

The dreaded Retakes.

I was always a Retake. I dressed up for Retake Day, like a nervous batter on a second strike. Retakes were a mark of kiddie shame. All of us baby trolls, lined up and dressed to the nines, when nobody else was. And no more free combs. They knew we weren't worth it. I would have been a Re-Retake if they had it, but there was only so much they could do, then.

Now, I'd ask to be retouched.

You have to be at least fifty years old to be Photoshopped.

In other words, only adults can act childish.

But those days are gone.

My school pictures, as bad as they were, are some of the forty pictures that exist of me, as a child. Kids today already have 7,384,747 photos taken of them, even before they get to Picture Day. In fact, kids have their own cameras, webcams, camera phones, and Flip videos.

Nowadays, kids get to be the Wizard of Oz.

And you know what?

That *is* progress.

Can This Marriage Be Saved?

|||||||||||||||||||||||||||||||||||||||||||||||||

By Lisa

Breaking up is hard to do, especially with a credit card company.

Our melodrama begins when I'm paying bills and notice a $50.00 balance on a credit card that I hadn't used in a long time. When I checked the statement, it said that the charge was the annual fee. I was wondering if I needed to pay fifty dollars for a card I didn't use when I clapped eyes on the interest rate.

30.24 percent.

Yes, you read that right. In other words, if I had a balance on the card at any time, they could charge me 30 percent more than the cost of all the stuff I bought.

Like a great sale, only in reverse.

I'm not stingy, but I could get money cheaper from The Mob.

I read further and saw that the Mafia, er, I mean, the credit card company, could also charge me a late fee of $39.95, which was undoubtedly a fair price for processing the transaction, as I bet their billing department is headed by Albert Einstein.

So I made a decision.

I called the customer service number, which was almost impossible to find on the statement, and as directed, plugged in my 85-digit account number. Of course, as soon as a woman answered the phone, the first question she asked was:

"What is your account number?"

I bit my tongue. They all ask this, and I always want to answer, "Why did you have me key it in? To make it harder to call customer service?"

Perish the thought.

So I told her I wanted to cancel the card, and her tone stiffened. She said, "May I ask why you wish to close your account?"

For starters, I told her about the annual fee.

"Would it make a difference if there were no annual fee?"

I wanted to answer, Is it that easy to disappear this annual fee, and if so, why do you extort it in the first place? But instead, I said only, "No, because you have a usurious interest rate and late fee."

"Will you hold while I transfer you to a Relationship Counselor?"

I'm not making this up. This is verbatim. You can divorce your hubby easier than you can divorce your VISA card. I said for fun, "Do I have a choice?"

"Please hold," she answered, and after a few clicks, a man came on the line.

"Thanks for patiently waiting," he purred. His voice was deep and sexy. His accent was indeterminate, but exotic, as if he were from the Country of Love.

Meow.

Suffice it to say that the Relationship Counselor got my immediate attention. I was beginning to think we could work on our relationship, and if we met twice a week, we could turn this baby around. He sounded like a combination of Fabio and George Clooney. You know who George Clooney is. If you don't know who Fabio is, you're not old enough to read what follows.

"No problem," I said. I did not say, What are you wearing?

"Please let me have your account number," he breathed, which almost killed the mood.

So I told him and said that I wanted to cancel my card.

"I'm sorry to hear that," he said. He sounded genuinely sad. I wanted to comfort him, and I knew exactly how.

But I didn't say that, because it would be inappropriate.

"I have a suggestion," he whispered.

So do I. Sign me up for 5 more cards. You have my number, all 85 digits.

"We can switch you to the no-fee card."

I came to my senses. "Can you switch me to the no-highway-robbery interest rate?"

"Pardon me?" he asked, but I didn't repeat it.

"Thanks, I just want to cancel the card."

"I understand. And I respect your decision."

He actually said that. I made up the 85 digits part, but the rest is absolutely true.

I knew what I wanted to say before I hung up. That we'd had a good run, but like a love meteor, we burned too hot, for too short a time.

Instead I said, "Thanks."

Honestly, it's not me.

It's you.

Meow

|||||||||||||||||||||||||||||||||||||||||||||||||||||

By Francesca

The other day, I was walking my dog, Pip, and talking to my mom on the phone, like I always do. Dog walking is prime time for calls home. I speak into headphones that are plugged into my cell, so I'm one of those people who appears to be talking to herself. But this is New York, so that's normal.

Anyway, I was halfway through my route, yapping away to my mom, when Pip shot in front of me, jerking the leash. Then he whipped around to face me, ears up, eyes wide, looking ready to jump into my arms like Scooby Doo. I turned around to see what had spooked him.

There stood a calico cat, back arched, tail bristling, green eyes glowering in our direction. So I thought: *Oh, silly Pip inadvertently startled this nice cat.*

The cat emitted a low, rumbling growl.

Correction: *Pip inadvertently startled this not-so-nice cat.*

The cat took several slow and deliberate steps toward us.

Okay, so this cat has an issue with dogs, maybe it was abused by a dog in its kittenhood. That's okay, I'll just take the dog out of the equation.

I picked Pip up and backed away, but the cat locked eyes with me. The farther I retreated, the faster the cat advanced.

I put on my best calm-assertive, dog-trainer voice and said, "Hey, hey, no. Bad cat. No!"

Someone tell Cesar Milan that what works on a pit bull does not work on a feisty feline. I was shocked when the cat yowled and took a swipe at my shin, after which point, I did the only sensible thing.

Turn tail and run.

So there I was, running down the sidewalk, clutching Pip to my chest like some refugee puppy, with the crazy cat chasing me. The entire thing was so absurd, I started laughing as I ran, which made me seem even more maniacal to the startled pedestrians as I streaked past.

Down the street at the corner, there was a giant puddle by the curb, and in it I saw my opportunity for escape. I leapt over the puddle in what could only be called a leap of faith, as Pip's flying ears obscured my vision. We didn't quite make it; my right foot landed in the edge of the puddle, splashing dirty street water all over myself.

Great.

But my water landing did succeed in thwarting Terminator Cat, who recoiled at the puddle and, with a twitchy kick of its hind leg, slunk back home to its lair.

"What is going on? Are you okay?" my mother's voice said in my ear.

I had completely forgotten that I still had my earbuds in and my mom on the phone. I did my best to tell her the story, winded and spitting dog hair out of my mouth. "I don't know what got the cat so mad! I love cats, and you know Pip, he never bothers the cats back home."

This last part was only half-true.

Pip looks shaken, not stirred.

"I'm sure you didn't do anything to provoke it," my mom said. "Some cats just want to take a swipe at you. Like that writing teacher."

"Huh?" I readjusted the headphone in my ear.

"That jerky writing professor, the one who was so mean to you."

Gotta love mom-bias. I remembered now; in college, it took me two years to screw up the courage to apply for a creative writing class. I got into a workshop with my first-choice professor—a smart female author and single mother to one daughter.

Sound familiar?

I was sure we would get along.

But we didn't.

Safe in Francesca's arms

I did everything I could to win her over. I arrived in class promptly, participated in discussion, devoted myself to each assignment, and turned pieces in on time, double-spaced, single-sided, Arial font, just like she'd asked.

Yet somehow, everything I said or did rubbed her the wrong way. Our troubles culminated on the day of my first story workshop, when she opened the discussion by decimating my piece. The awkward silence that followed her diatribe was impenetrable; no one in the class wanted to say anything. We were dismissed early.

Now, don't get me wrong. I can take criticism. I'm a big girl.

So I waited until I was in the privacy of my dorm room to cry.

"Yeah, that wasn't really one of the high points of college, Mom. I ended up dropping the class, remember?"

"I do remember. However, didn't you find out later that four other students in her advanced workshop had also dropped the class?"

"Actually, I think it was five."

"Right. And dropping it wasn't all you did. The next semester, you got into another workshop with the department head. And a year later, you graduated with honors and a novel as your award-winning thesis."

Yes, my mom brags about me, to me.

Aren't moms the best?

"So what I think you're saying is the cat today was an assassin sent by my disgruntled writing professor? A hired hit-cat!"

"The point is," she continued, "you believed in yourself. Not everyone will like you. Some people just want to take swipes at you. You need to trust yourself enough to ignore them."

Or at least have a mother who loves you enough to pick you up and run away.

Holy Moly

|||||||||||||||||||||||||||||||||||||||||||||||||||||||

By Lisa

I have a mole on my butt. I'm telling you, but I can't bring myself to tell my dermatologist.

Ironic, no?

Maybe he'll read this, give me a call, and tell me I need to come in. And I'll get an appointment before 2023.

I go to my dermatologist every year, for a mole checkup. He puts on a visor that magnifies his eyes to the size of brown golf balls, then he rolls them all over my body, scanning my skin for bad-news moles. So far, so good. All my moles are harmless. In fact, they're adorable, and I think my stomach sports the Big and Little Dippers.

During my annual mole checkups, I lie down on the padded table and yap away, so I feel less self-conscious. I'm a champ at yapping away during medical exams. At the gynecologist, I'm Chatty Cathy.

I conduct monologues when any doctor examines me, for anything. I filibuster if I'm naked, but also if I'm not. As soon as that stethoscope goes inside my blouse, I start talking about the weather. My doctors go home at night with massive headaches from listening to me, their brains swimming with relative humidity, barometric pressure, and whether this winter will be as bad as the last.

Cold enough for you?

The other thing I do during medical exams is avert my eyes, especially when my gynecologist is palpating my breasts for lumps. I bet I'm not alone in this. Whether your gynecologist is male or female, when he or she is examining your breasts, I bet you avert your eyes like crazy.

You have to. If you look at them, it's sex.

When I'm getting a breast exam, I avert, avert, avert. I look around the examining room as if it's the first time I've been to the United States. Wow, look at that chair! And what is that, a desk? And there's a telephone!

Jeez, what will they think of next?

And all the while, I'm chatting away. Cold front. Warm front. My front.

I shift my monologue into high gear during my pap smear. As soon I get my feet in the stirrups, I'm the Weather Channel. And when that speculum shows up, I add a news and traffic report.

But to stay on point, I'd just had my yearly mole check-up, and my dermatologist didn't find my butt mole because you don't have to take your underwear off for the exam. I don't know why. Maybe they think you can't get a bad-news mole on your butt, because it never sees the sun. Except that mine does, every time I bend over in my jeans, for that oh-so-attractive muffin-top spillage.

Now there's a visual.

Plumber's butt isn't limited to plumbers, if you follow.

So I have a mole and a problem. I should just call the dermatologist, but I'm not sure the mole is anything to be worried about or if it's even new. I have no idea when it got there, much less when it took up residence. I mean, how often do you look at your own naked butt?

Too personal?

If you said yes, you're new around here.

We all ask does-this-make-my-butt-look-big when we put on a pair of jeans, but not many of us are looking at our butts, in the buff. That kind of behavior makes navel-gazing look tame.

The safe thing to do is call the doctor and get an appointment, and I probably will, but what do I say? Put differently, do I want to be the creepy patient who insists that the doctor look at my butt?

I didn't know what to do, so I told Daughter Francesca, and she told me to go tell the dermatologist. But I thought she was being alarmist, so I told two of my girlfriends, and they both agreed with Francesca. In fact, one of them had a butt mole of her own, and so did her daughter.

One needed surgery.

Yikes.

So I'm calling. And before I go, I'm checking the weather report.

I have to bone up on the humidity.

Cover Me

By Lisa

I don't know who invented duvet covers, but judging from the spelling, it was the French, and I'm guessing they did it in retaliation for Pepé Le Pew.

Oo-la-la, mon cheri.

I don't know when I got sucked into the duvet-cover scam, but I think it was in the eighties, a time before I had dogs, which is relevant here. Because back then, the duvet cover never needed washing, and everything was fine. But now I have to wash it all the time, as a result of sleeping with various and sundry critters, which means that I have to put it back on the bed again.

And it's just impossible to put a duvet cover back on a duvet, or if we stop being pretentious, a comforter.

I don't know how to do it in less than an hour. And last time, I got so disgusted that I gave up and just placed the duvet cover on top of the comforter, making my bed like a cheese sandwich.

I mean, what's the difference? The cover was covering the duvet, after all, and who's coming after me? The gendarmerie?

I simply can't do it.

Here's my procedure: I stuff the corner of the comforter in

one corner of the duvet cover, then jump up on the bed and shake the comforter down the sides and into the other corners, which is when I realize I have the comforter twisted like a double helix inside the cover. So then I have to dump the comforter out and start all over again while profanity commences, and I forget about bothering with whether the comforter is lengthwise or not, because I pretend it's a square. Bottom line, I struggle and struggle until the comforter is shoved back inside the cover, like a baby stuffed back into its amniotic sac, a process that's only slightly less painful than giving birth in reverse.

If you follow.

I'm over it. I'm done with duvet covers and the other impossible things around my house, like halogen bulbs. I have them under my kitchen cabinets, and the contractor swore to me they would be beautiful, and they are. But he never told me that it would be impossible to change the itsy-bitsy, teeny-weeny, twenty-watt, double-pronged bulb.

And by the way, you're not allowed to touch it with your fingers.

I'm not kidding.

He told me that the oil from my fingertips will somehow rub off on the glass of the halogen bulb and cause it to spontaneously combust or perhaps cause World War III, and that I'm supposed to take a paper towel or piece of toilet paper, wrap it around the halogen bulb, then hold the wrapped bulb between my thumb and index finger and stick that assembly in the pinpoint holes in the fixture.

Try this at home.

The bulb will pop like a cork from the paper towel, sail

through the air, land on the counter, and shatter into lethal shards. It will take four bulbs to get one inside.

You'll see.

Or, if you manage to keep your grip on the paper-and-bulb combo, try sticking the bulb's two prongs, which are the gauge of sewing needles and just as pointy, into the tiny holes in the fixture, which are the size of a needle's eye.

Good luck with that. You could attach a spaceship to a docking station with greater ease.

And the kicker is that since my fixture is under the cabinet, I have to bend backwards in order to change the bulb, so that the back of my head is resting on the counter. Then I try to stick the bulb in the fixture, like a mechanic under a car, only doing the limbo. The last time I changed a bulb, I felt like I ripped my stomach muscles. It gave new meaning to shredded abs.

So I tried a new way, climbing onto my counter and lying down under the cabinets like I was going to sleep. I went through two bulbs and gave up, and now I'm cursing the halogen bulb and the duvet cover.

And Pepé Le Pew.

Mother Mary and
The Retirement Village

|||||||||||||||||||||||||||||||||||||||||||||||||

By Lisa

Sooner or later, most families will deal with the question of whether an aging mom or dad should move to a retirement community. The pamphlets say it's not an easy decision, and they never met Mother Mary.

We begin with some background.

As you may know, my mother lives with Brother Frank in South Beach, and lately they've been talking about selling their house.

By lately, I mean the past twenty years.

The Flying Scottolines move slowly. So slowly, in fact, that we try to sell houses in the worst recession of all time, in which the real estate prices are at an all-time low. If you need investment advice, just ask us. We hear that tech stocks are superhot.

If Mother Mary and Brother Frank sell their house, the question becomes whether they should continue to live together, or whether Mother Mary should move to a retirement village.

It takes a village to raise Mother Mary.

And I wish it luck.

Anyway, they can't decide what to do. They love living together. He's gay, and his gay friends love their moms, so they're all living in a happy circle of fragrant stereotypes.

And Frank takes wonderful care of her, taking her to all of her doctor's appointments, grocery store runs, and occasional dinners out. There's a special place in heaven reserved for people who take such great care of their parents, and once my brother gets there, he'll not only get a free pass, he'll be allowed to park anywhere.

By the way, Mother Mary doesn't want to live with me, because she says, "All you do is read and write."

To which I plead guilty.

And though we prefer her to live with family, we all know that Frank might not always be able to take care of her, and that even though she's in great health now, she might not always be. So we're all confused, and I decided that we should go visit a retirement village near me in Pennsylvania, since none of us had ever seen one. In fact, we're so old-school that we kept calling it a "nursing home," which is the last term that applies.

On the contrary, it's paradise.

We were shown through a lovely building, complete with two restaurants and a "pub," which serves drinks in front of a big TV. We read a daily menu that included trout almandine, duck with wild rice, and baked Alaska. We toured a gym that had a Jacuzzi and an indoor pool. We saw a beautiful one-bedroom apartment with freshly painted walls, cushy wool rugs, and maid service. We got brochures on discount trips to Egypt and London. And they have a computer class, a book club, canasta, bridge, and pinochle clubs, plus yoga, aerobics, free weights, and "seated" exercise.

So you know where this is going:

I'm ready to move in.

Now.

Say the word.

Retire me.

I'm old enough, at least I feel old enough.

They had me at "seated exercise." Exercising while seated is my kind of exercise. It's a piece a cake.

Just do it.

For example, I'm seated right now, watching football on TV, which I gather is "unseated exercise." How conventional. All that moving around.

Who needs it?

But to stay on point, I fell in love with the place, and so did Brother Frank. It even had a huge model train set, which he began playing with immediately, pressing the button to make the toy locomotive chug through the fake forest, until it derailed, careened off the track, and vanished into some fake shrubbery.

He walked away quickly.

I blamed it on my mother.

Why not? It's the American way.

And I bet you think you know what Mother Mary thought of the place.

She loved it.

Surprise!

She's hasn't decided she wants to move there, and they're going back to Florida to let it sink in. We'll see what happens, and I'll let you know. I'm just happy that she didn't reject the idea outright.

I think they had her at "maid service."

The Suburbs Are Killing Me

||||||||||||||||||||||||||||||||||||||||||||||||||

By Francesca

Many people believe that cities are dangerous places, and they're not entirely wrong. There are higher crime rates, cabs speeding around corners, shaky scaffolding, fizzling car bombs, uncovered manholes, bedbugs, and pianos being delivered via deteriorating rope.

But does that make a place unsafe?

I'll tell you about unsafe.

This summer, the suburbs almost killed me.

And not in the figurative sense. I mean the suburbs were actually, physically, beating me up.

That may sound ridiculous, but let me give you the facts: a perfectly healthy twentysomething went home to the 'burbs and ended up in the emergency room four times.

It began when I came home one long weekend in July. I was walking around in my backyard when CRACK! I stepped in a hole and heard my big toe break. Who had booby-trapped the yard?

Ruby, the dog.

Unlike municipal construction workers, dogs don't string CAUTION tape around their worksites.

My foot ballooned, and I agreed with my mother that I ought

to get it checked out. We went to the emergency room, and I explained how I broke my toe, a story with the panache of slipping on a banana peel.

I had yet to recognize the cunning of the suburbs lies in its ho-hum façade.

This same weekend, a storm knocked out our power at home. With the temperatures in the nineties every day, I thought the worst of the outage was the lack of fans and air-conditioning. But it was evening, and there were no lights in the house, and I was looking for my cell phone. I spotted it on the floor, bent to get it, and WHAM! I hit my head on a shelf and knocked myself out.

The ER nurse looked at my chart and frowned. "Your record says . . . you were here yesterday? Is this a related incident?"

I felt like an idiot. No, ma'am, yesterday I stepped in a hole, today I hit my head on a shelf. Oh, the banality!

At least when you're mugged in the city you have a story to tell.

I was treated for a concussion and in a few days I hobbled back to Manhattan, nursing a headache and a limp.

But the blow to the head must have damaged my memory, because by August, I returned home for a week of staycation. One day, my mom and I joined some friends for a horseback ride. We were cantering out in the open field with the sun on our backs and the wind in our hair. My horse must've felt the thrill too, because he bucked, and the next thing I knew, I was feeling the wind everywhere else. Sailing through the air, I had only enough time to think, "Oh, dear," before I ate dirt.

Emergency room visit number three.

The last thing Francesca saw before she ate dirt

Thankfully, my second brain scan of the summer showed no damage to my noggin—thanks to my helmet—and a slide-show of X-rays to my back and pelvis showed no breaks. My pain was severe soft-tissue damage that would heal with time.

The suburbs know better than to leave a mark.

So they loaded me up with prescriptions for Vicodin and a muscle relaxant, and sent me home.

Exactly one week later, I woke up with terrible stomach pain. I went to my regular doctor, but he couldn't pinpoint the cause. He said he would need a CAT scan of my body to rule out ailments like appendicitis. Of course, there's only one place that provides that kind of equipment without an appointment.

At the emergency room check-in desk, the woman looked up and smiled. "Francesca, right?"

You wanna go, where everybody knows your name . . .

Four hours later, my new friends at the ER concluded that I was experiencing a bad reaction to my pain medication.

Popping painkillers—the quintessential suburban sin. How did I, a single twenty-four-year-old who lives in the city, become a desperate housewife? And where is my sexy, shirtless gardener?

But the real question is, how did the cocoon of my childhood become a house of pain? Are the suburbs kicking me out? I don't know what's going on.

All I know is that I need to get back to the city.

Where it's safe.

The Mothership

|||||||||||||||||||||||||||||||||||||||||||||||||

By Lisa

I'm a terrible negotiator. I'm too emotional, and I can't pretend I don't want something I really want.

Like George Clooney.

But today we're talking cars, and this is the tale of my first attempt at negotiating.

To begin, I have an older car that I take great care of, and it's aged better than I have, sailing past 100,000 miles without estrogen replacement.

But around 102,000 miles, things started to go wrong, and flaxseed wasn't helping. I knew I'd be driving long distances on book tour, and I started to worry. I called up my genius assistant Laura to ask her advice, as I do before I make any important decision, like what to eat for lunch.

I asked her, "Laura, do you think I need a new car?"

"Yes. Absolutely."

"But it's paid off, and I love it." And I do. It's a big white sedan called The Mothership.

"I know, but you have to be safe. What if it breaks down on tour?"

"That won't happen."

"Except it has. Twice."

An excellent point. One time, The Mothership died on the way to a bookstore in Connecticut, requiring the bookseller to pick me up at a truck-stop on I-95. I bet that never happened to James Patterson.

So I needed a new car, and since I love my dealership, I went there. I thought they loved me, too, which they did, except when it came to the bottom line. They gave me a good deal on a new SUV, but a rock-bottom price on trading in The Mothership.

I asked, "How can you do that to her? I mean, me?"

I told you I get too emotional.

And I added, "Plus you're supposed to love me."

But they don't. They run a business, and it's not the love business. However, it's my secret philosophy that all business is the love business, so I got angry. They had taken care of The Mothership for the past ten years, at top dollar, and it was worth so much more.

Guess what I did.

I walked out.

I took my business elsewhere. That very day, I called up another dealership, who said, come on over, we love you, too. In fact, we love you so much that we'll give you a better deal on your trade-in. And they did, after inspecting The Mother-ship and calling her "the cleanest 100,000-mile car they had ever seen," which we are.

I mean, it is.

But just when I was about to say yes, my old dealership called and told me that they still loved me. I told them I was already rebounding with my new dealership, but they said they'd top the offer on The Mothership, and after much back-and-forth, I went back to my old dealership, like ex sex.

But long story short, the day came when I was supposed to pick up my new SUV, and I felt unaccountably sad. I took final pictures of The Mothership. I stalled leaving the house. On the drive to the dealer, I called Daughter Francesca and asked her, "Wanna say good-bye to the car?"

"Mom? You don't sound happy."

"I'm not. I love this car."

"Aww, it's okay. It's probably not the car, anyway. It's that you have such great memories in the car."

I considered this for a minute. "No, it's the car."

By the time I reached the dealership, I was crying full bore, snot included.

My sales guy came over, and when he saw me, his smile faded. "What's the matter?"

"I love my car. I don't want to give it up."

"So keep it," he said, which was the first time it even occurred to me. I know it sounds dumb, but it simply never entered my mind. I'd never bought a car without trading one in.

"But what about the money?"

"We're only offering you a fraction of what the car's worth. If I were you, I'd keep it."

"But I'm only one person. Why do I need two cars?"

"They're two different cars. The old one's a sedan, and the new one's an SUV."

I wiped my eyes. "You mean, like shoes? This is the dressy pair?"

He looked nonplussed. "Uh, right."

"Really?" My heart leapt with happiness. I decided to keep The Mothership. It's strappy sandals on wheels, if you follow.

Thus ended my first attempt at hardball negotiations, which backfired. Having bargained for the best price on a trade-in, I couldn't bring myself to trade anything in.

Because I love it.

It sits in my garage, aging happily.

Soon we'll both be antique.

Priceless.

Brush Off

|||||||||||||||||||||||||||||||||||||||||||||||||||

By Lisa

I just read an article about women who pay $168 to have their bodies brushed.

Good to know. I'd been looking for a new way to blow $168, and now I have one.

Turns out you can go to a spa, get naked, and have your entire body brushed with hard bristles.

A pap smear sounds like more fun to me.

The article said that you can also buy a brush and start brushing your skin at home. One woman said it was like a "morning cup of coffee."

Also good to know.

To me, the only thing like a morning cup of coffee is a morning cup of coffee. But I've been narrow-minded. The woman in the article brushes her skin every morning.

I don't even brush my hair every morning.

Evidently, brushing the skin was an ancient ritual in Japan and Greece. I didn't know that either, but to me, that doesn't necessarily mean it's a good idea. For example, another ancient ritual from Japan is foot-binding. And one from ancient Greece is democracy.

Look where that got us.

One woman in the article goes regularly to a spa for a body brushing, which she does "to get the toxins out."

Again, with the toxins.

I've read enough about toxins. Everybody's talking about toxins. To get rid of toxins, people go on fasts, where they don't eat for a week, or they get colonics, which I'm not going to explain herein.

You can figure it out. People who read are smart.

Smart enough to avoid colonics.

But here's my question: What toxins do they need to get out of their bodies, and how did the toxins get inside?

In the article, the spa owner said that her clients think, "If I eat a bunch of cheese, and eat a bunch of chocolate cake, it will go to my face or my rear, and I need to go detox."

Again. Wow!

I'm no scientist, so I didn't know that chocolate cake was toxic. I've eaten tons of chocolate cake in my lifetime, because it's my favorite food, and it's never poisoned me. Or at least I don't think it has, but you never know. I'm keeping my eye on chocolate cake, from now on.

Plus I never knew you needed to detox from chocolate cake. I always thought you needed to detox if you took heroin. But chocolate cake isn't addictive.

Oh, wait.

Still.

Even if it were, I didn't realize that brushing your skin would cure you. I thought that the only thing you could do with a brush that would cure you of chocolate cake was to stick it in your mouth.

The brush, not the cake.

And you'll be happy to know that the spa has a treatment they call FatGirlSlim, which includes body brushing, and another woman says she brushes her body "to stay thin."

Whoa.

Who knew that brushing your skin would make you thin? I thought you had to diet and exercise to lose weight, but that's old news, I guess. It seems a lot easier to wake up and brush my body, and I intend to start. After all, I brush my teeth every morning, why not my skin? Then I'll be MiddleAgedSkinny.

Finally, the article reports that women are now brushing their butts, in the hope that their cellulite will disappear.

I could have told you that would happen. If I thought it would get rid of my cellulite, I'd buy an orbital sander.

The spa owner insists that brushing gets rid of cellulite, but some doctor says it doesn't. Nothing like a medical degree to kill the buzz.

And he says that body brushing can put the skin at risk for inflammation, redness and an itchy rash.

Clearly, he needs a spanking.

With a brush.

Love and Worry

||||||||||||||||||||||||||||||||||||||||||||||||||

By Lisa

I have a scientific theory that the bonds that tie mothers and daughters are love and worry, like the two strands in the double helix of some very twisty DNA.

In other words, if I love you, I worry about you. And vice versa.

Let me explain.

The moment Daughter Francesca was born, I started to love and worry about her. And my worry, like my love, had no bounds. I worried if she was sleeping too much. I worried if she was sleeping too little. Same with crying, nursing, and pooping. If I was breathing, I was loving, and worrying. And my biggest worry, of course, was whether she was breathing. I'm not the only mother who has watched her baby sleeping to see if her chest goes up and down.

I still do that.

My theory also applies to grandmothers. Because they're mothers, too. Just grander.

Mother Mary worried about Francesca, and all of our conversations back then were consumed with my worries and hers, and together we aimed our laser beams of worry on this hapless infant, which is undoubtedly why she turned out so great.

Or guilty.

But that's not the point, herein.

The point is that Francesca knows we worried about her. Uh, I mean, we loved her.

Likewise, I know, in turn, that Mother Mary worries about me. She worries that I work too hard. She worries when I fly. She worries when I drive. She worries when I'm not at home, and even more when I am at home. For example, she worries that I could put too much food on my fork and choke.

Let me suggest that this last worry isn't so dumb. You've never seen me eat.

I used to feel guilty that she worried about me, but now I don't.

She should worry about me, constantly.

It proves she loves me.

I realized this when I understood how much I still worried about Francesca, even though she's living in New York, on her own. I don't mean to make her feel guilty, and she shouldn't. But I can't help it.

Motherhood has no expiration date, right?

And what just happened is that the worry has boomeranged, so that I'm starting to worry about Mother Mary.

Well, not starting.

But recently my worry, and my love, has come to the fore, because of Mother Mary's health. In particular, her nose.

It's blue.

No joke. The last time she came to visit, the first thing that I noticed was that her nose had a distinctly bluish tinge. I told her so, in a nice way, and she told me to shut up.

But still, I worried, big-time. Her circulation has never been good, due to a lifetime of smoking, but she finally quit at age 82, when she got throat cancer.

Better late than never.

Anyway, she beat cancer, which is remarkable enough, but she's supposed to use oxygen at night, according to her doctor. But she won't do it. Our conversation today on the phone went like this:

"Ma, why won't you use your oxygen?"

"I don't like the tube. It smells like popcorn."

"So what? Popcorn is good. Who doesn't like popcorn?"

"I don't, and that's what it smells like, so forget it."

"But it's doctor's orders, Ma."

"The doctor? What does *he* know?"

I don't know where to begin. "Everything?"

Motherhood has no expiration date.

But Mother Mary wouldn't listen, even though I eventually raised my voice, which is another thing that mothers/daughters do to prove our love.

If I'm yelling at you, you know I love you.

Because I want your chest to keep going up and down, whether you're my daughter or my mother.

Or whether I'm your daughter or your mother.

It's all the same emotion, which is worry.

Or love!

So the next time your mother is worried about you, don't tell her to shut up.

And don't feel guilty either.

Try and understand. She can't help it. It's in her DNA.

Chalk it up to mom genes.

Getting It Straight

||||||||||||||||||||||||||||||||||||||||||||||||||

By Lisa

Women have come a long way, baby, except for one thing: Hair.

By which I mean, curly or straight?

Secretly, I have curly hair, and not wavy curly, I'm talking majorly curly. I don't have curls, I have coils. I don't have naturally curly hair, I have unnaturally curly hair.

Let me take you back in time, to the Jurassic.

By which I mean, 1955.

When I was little, I had so many curls that once they sprouted from my head, they grew sideways, defying many natural laws, starting with gravity. Bottom line, on my shoulders sat a triangle of hair.

I was too small to care. If anything, I thought it was good, because every adult who came up to me asked, "Where did you get that curly hair?"

Let's pause a moment to examine the questions we ask little kids.

I had no idea where I got my curly hair or my blue eyes. Nor did I know the answer to the third question, which was usually, "Do you help your mommy in the kitchen?"

I swear, this happened. There was a time in America when

they asked little girls this question, all the time. Now, they're not allowed to. It's against federal law. Try it, and go to politically correct jail.

Nowadays, nobody's in the kitchen, and we're all overweight.

Anyway, I got older, and kids started to tease me about my hair. All the cool girls in school had straight hair, as did the girls on TV and in magazines. Also my best friend Rachel, whom I loved.

So I discovered Dippity-Do. It was hair goop, and they still make it. I checked online and found the website, where they claim to be "the original name in gels, for over 45 years."

Bingo.

I seem to remember that Dippity-Do came in pink or blue, maybe for girls or boys, but that could be my imagination. Boys didn't use it, anyway, because they liked themselves the way they were, which was clearly insane.

Girls used Dippity-Do by the tubful, and by ninth grade, I had mastered the art of slathering it all over my wet head, putting my hair on top of my head in a ponytail, and wrapping it around a Maxwell House coffee can, which I bobby-pinned to my scalp.

Then I tried to sleep.

If American girls were drowsy in math class, this was the reason. My hair didn't even look good, because it would be bumpy on top, until it fell out. The sides would be smooth, except for telltale ridges from the coffee can. And the delicious aroma of Maxwell House.

Still, I did not stop, as there was another product to try, which there always is, this being America, where we girls know that if we just buy X, we'll be beautiful and our lives will change.

I'm talking U.N.C.U.R.L. It was some kind of chemical straightener that you painted on your hair while holding your nose.

It had great marketing, with a spy-girl on the front of the box, and if you bought it, you became "The Girl From U.N.C.U.R.L.," which would make you feel like a cool double agent and not a miserable preteen with a triangle head.

The stuff smelled funny but worked great.

For two days.

Then came blowdryers, and the rest is history. We could blow our hair straight, using an array of gels and mousses, and I still do, though it's starting to seem like too much work. Once, on book tour, I got too tired to blowdry my hair, and my then-publicist looked at me in horror.

"What did you do to your hair?" she asked, aghast.

"I let it go curly," I answered, in ninth grade again.

She said, "But you don't look like your author photo."

I blinked. That I knew already. I look nothing like my author photo. That's the whole point of an author photo. If it looked like the author, nobody would buy the book.

The girl in my author photo is from U.N.C.U.R.L.

In contrast, Daughter Francesca was born with curls, lived through all the dumb questions people asked her, and always wore her curls with pride.

"Mom, why don't you wear your hair curly?" she said to me, the other day, and I told her this whole story. And she said, gently, "I think you should just be yourself."

I'm considering it, and we'll see.

Sometimes it takes a kid to straighten out a mom.

The Heart of a Gambler

||||||||||||||||||||||||||||||||||||||||||||||||||

By Francesca

Recently, two friends and I decided to break free from our everyday lives and escape to Atlantic City for the weekend. None of us had ever really gambled before, but we were feeling lucky.

But, as we wandered through the maze-like casino floor, our confidence dissipated faster than cigarette smoke. Poker was way too intimidating. Slots seemed like a hopeless long shot. Between the three of us, we know all the words to *Guys and Dolls,* but our collective understanding of craps consisted of "seven is good."

When faced with forking over our hard-earned, first-job cash, we didn't want to risk it.

"I don't think we're cut out for this," my friend said. "We don't have the right personality for gambling."

I wondered if she was right. Am I always this risk-averse? What do I consider a worthy gamble?

The answer came quickly.

Love.

When it comes to romance, I take my chances. Consider it high-stakes emotional poker. And what's my weakness?

Ex-boyfriends.

I always give them a second chance, or third, or fourth to make it work. Despite all evidence to the contrary, I think, "the next time, this could really turn around."

I'd like to think I'm an optimist. But deep down, I might have the heart of a gambler.

This time last year, I made my greatest romantic gamble. I had broken up with this guy years before, and we had barely spoken since, but he had remained a little ache in my heart. After attending a friend's wedding, I was infused with enough sentimentality and champagne to fire off an email telling him how I felt.

Turned out, he felt the same way.

Not content to quit while I was ahead, I agreed to visit him on his military base. He's training to be a fighter pilot, dreamy uniform included.

See why it's hard for me to get over him?

I blame Tom Cruise.

All of my friends warned me the trip was a bad idea. My mom's take was a little different: "If you feel like you need to do it, do it. You can handle whatever happens."

Never bet more than you have to lose.

So I did it. I packed more cosmetic toiletries than federally allowed and hopped two planes to see him. We spent a week catching up and generally feeling like no time had passed. It took me all of twelve hours to fall for him again.

Before I knew it, I was all in.

But as luck would have it, on the last day, he told me it couldn't work.

If you're going to cry in a public place, an airport that serves a major military base is the place to be. Every airport employee and many passersby offered sympathetic smiles and words of comfort. The TSA employee at security even gave me a hug, though he still made me throw out my scented body lotion.

I felt guilty accepting their kindness, but I didn't have the heart to correct them that I wasn't a serviceman's sweetheart, I'd just been dumped.

But I survived. I came home to my wonderful family and friends who swallowed their I-told-you-so's and met me with support and understanding. And even while nursing a broken heart and a bruised ego, I felt satisfied. I had said the unsaid, laid my cards on the table, and taken my chance.

It was my last great gamble, a loss, and yet I'd do it over again.

With that in mind, casino games seemed like child's play.

My friends and I finally agreed that blackjack was easy enough for our comfort level. With beginner's luck, we won the first three hands. On the fourth, we were dealt a low number, thirteen. High off our previous wins, we decided to take our chances.

"Hit me!"

Ten of clubs. Twenty-three. We lose.

The player next to us snapped, "Why didn't you stay? The odds were against you. That was so stupid!"

The dealer, an older woman, shot the player a dirty look. Then she pointed a red-nailed finger in our direction and said, "Honey, don't listen to him. That is *your* hand. You go ahead and play it however you want to."

Couldn't have said it better myself.

Clipped

||||||||||||||||||||||||||||||||||||||||||||||||||

By Lisa

If you raise your daughter right, eventually she will know more than you. Which is the good and bad news.

We begin when Daughter Francesca comes home for a visit and finds me engaged in one of my more adorable habits, which is clipping my fingernails over the trashcan in the kitchen.

This would be one of the benefits of being an empty nester. You can do what you want, wherever you want. The house is all yours.

Weee!

In my case, this means that everything that I should properly do in my bathroom, I do in my kitchen.

Except one thing.

Please.

I keep it classy.

Bottom line, I wash my face and brush my teeth in the kitchen. I'm writing on my laptop in the kitchen, right now. My game plan is to live no more than three steps from the refrigerator at all times, which gives you an idea of my priorities.

Francesca eyes me with daughterly concern. "What are you doing?"

"Making sure the clippings don't go all over the floor," I tell her, clipping away. Each snip produces a satisfying *clik*.

"It's not good for your nails, to clip them that way. You might want to use an emery board."

I know she learned that from Mother Mary, who carries an emery board everywhere, like a concealed weapon. "I don't have one."

"I do, and you can use it."

"No, thanks. It's too much trouble." I keep clipping. *Clik, clik.* Hard little half-moons of fingernail fly into the trash. My aim is perfect, and wait'll I get to my toenails. Then I prop my foot up on the trash can and shoot the clippings into the air. Now *that's* entertainment.

She adds, gently, "You clip them kind of short."

"I know. So I don't have to do it so often."

"But your nails would look so pretty if you let them grow longer."

"I don't care enough."

Francesca looks a little sad. "I could do them for you, Mom. Shape them, polish them. Give you a nice manicure. Look at mine. I do it myself."

So I look up, and her hands are lovely, with each fingernail nicely shaped and lacquered with a hip, dark polish. It reminds me that I used to do my nails when I was her age. I used to care about my nails, but now I don't, and I'm not sure why I stopped. Either I'm mature, or slovenly.

"Thanks, but no," I tell her.

She seems disappointed. It is a known fact that parents will occasionally let their children down, and this will most often occur in the area of personal grooming or bad puns. I'm guilty of only one of these. All of my puns are good.

But to make a long story short, later we decide to go out to dinner, and since it's a nice night, I put on a pair of peep-toe shoes, which are shoes that reveal what's now known as toe cleavage, a term I dislike.

If your toe has cleavage, ask your plastic surgeon for a refund.

Anyway, both Francesca and I looked down at my unvarnished toenails, newly clipped though they were. I had to acknowledge that it wasn't a good look.

"I can polish them for you," she offered, with hope. "I think they would look better, with these shoes."

"But we're late," I said, and we were.

"It won't take long." Francesca reached for the nail polish, and I kicked off the shoes.

"I have an idea. Just do the ones that show."

"What?" Francesca turned around in surprise, nail polish in hand.

"Do the first three toenails."

Look, it made sense at the time. The other two toenails didn't matter, and no one can find my pinky toenail, which has withered away to a sliver, evidently on a diet more successful than mine.

But Francesca looked pained. "Please, let me do them all. We have time, and it's cheesy to only do the ones that show. It's like sweeping dirt under the rug."

So I gave in. Like I said, I raised her right.

Mother Mary Hears The Worst

|||||||||||||||||||||||||||||||||||||||||||||||||||||

By Lisa

The best way to deliver bad news is to be direct, so when Mother Mary answers the phone, I tell her right away: "Ma, are you sitting down? Because they canceled *Law & Order.*"

She scoffs. "That's not funny."

"I'm not kidding."

"Yes, you are."

"No, I'm not," I say. I know there are five stages of grief, and the first is denial, so I had fully expected her reaction. She watches *Law & Order* all day long. Anytime I call her, I hear *ba-bum* in the background. Also, she has a crush on Jerry Orbach, and I don't have the heart to tell her he's been canceled, too.

"This can't be true," she says in disbelief. "Everybody loves *Law & Order.*"

No, Everybody Loves Raymond, I think but don't say. "It was on for twenty years, so it lived a lot longer than most TV shows."

"Stop it. I know you're joking. You'll never fool me again."

She's referring to the one practical joke I played in my life, to wit: She loves the lottery, and during my broke days when I was trying to become a writer, she encouraged me to buy a lottery ticket. This would be your basic Scottoline plan for financial success, and who could blame her, because she used to win all the time, like $500 a pop. So once, when the Powerball got up to two million bucks, I called her and told her I'd bought a ticket but I'd missed when they'd read the winning number.

So you know where this is going.

I read her the winning number, slowly, digit by digit, and by the time I got to the fifth, I thought she was going to have a heart attack. This was thirty years ago, and she has never forgotten. Forgiving was never in her vocabulary in the first place. To Mother Mary, forgiveness is for the weak.

I try again. "I swear, it's the truth. Think of it this way. You'll always have the reruns."

"It's not the same," she says, finally believing me. She sounds so sad, my heart goes out to her.

"I'm sorry, Ma."

"How can they do that? They're so stupid!" she said, angry, which I know is the second stage of grief, and probably the one where she feels most comfy.

"Well, I guess they know." I want to move on to more important subjects, like her health. She's supposed to be on oxygen therapy at night, but Brother Frank told me she hadn't been cooperating. "Ma, how come you're not using your oxygen?"

"I don't want to."

"You have to. The doctor said." I was worried. The doctor found that her oxygen levels are too low, which surprises no one but her. We Scottolines have big noses, and she always says we get more oxygen than anybody in the room. Turns out one of us doesn't. "You need the oxygen, for your blood."

Are you sitting down?

"No, I don't."

"Yes, you do."

"Oh. Maybe . . . I do," she says, pausing.

I don't understand. "What?"

"It's probably nothing, but the other night, I got a pain in my arm."

Oh my God. "Ma, you did? Your upper arm? Your left arm?"

"Yes. How did you know?"

"That's a sign of a heart attack!"

She scoffed. "No, it's not."

"Yes, it is."

"You're joking. You think I'm stupid? My heart's not in my arm."

"Ma, really—" I stop when I hear her burst into laughter. "That's not funny."

She can't stop laughing. "Yes, it is, cookie."

And she's still laughing, when we hang up.

Half-Full

||||||||||||||||||||||||||||||||||||||||||||||||||||||||

By Lisa

I just read in the newspaper that an Italian lingerie manufacturer has instituted a program whereby women can return their used padded bras to the stores to be recycled into insulation for home construction.

Bravissimo!

I was wondering if this would work in the United States, but I don't think so. Why?

We don't throw out our old bras.

I don't have evidence on which to base my opinion, but I bet I'm right. I confirmed my theory by asking my girlfriends if they throw out their old bras. All of them agreed with me, which is why we have girlfriends.

I cannot throw away an old bra. I don't know why. Even if I don't wear it anymore, I keep my old bras in my drawer, where they ball up in a tangle of frayed lace, spent elastic, and underwires that could put out an eye.

I can tell the oldest ones because they're black and red, a veritable checkerboard of youthful enthusiasm. And they're made of nylon or some sheer synthetic that was eventually replaced by good old-fashioned white cotton, like an old Maidenform commercial.

From the days of maidens.

One of my friends does exactly what I do. Rather than throw away her old bras when her drawer gets too full, she simply starts a new drawer. And she buys new bras more often than I do, as she has a more active personal life, if you follow. I don't get a new bra unless I get a new husband.

So right now, I have ex-bras.

I don't know why my friends and I save our bras, except that it may have to do with the price. I remember when a bra cost twelve dollars. Now, you need a second mortgage, especially if it's what we used to call padded, which they now call formed. And instead of the soft cottony stuff they used to pad them with, they now use removable things called cutlets, which you can stuff in your bra if you like wearing veal.

I like the old padding better, of course. I have one bra that's padded with some sort of airy honeycomb. It used to make a minefield of bumps on my sweater, telling the world that not only I was wearing a padded bra, I was keeping bees.

The price of bras reaches its peak with a brand known as La Perla. The more financially prudent among you might not know about La Perla, so you'll have to trust me on this, as you should in all things. I've never lied to you, and will tell you now that a La Perla bra cost as much as a strand of pearlas.

How I came to possess a La Perla is a boring story, but the short of it is that I was going on TV, and the saleswoman told me I needed a special bra for TV, so I tried it on and it fit me like a cupcake pan in which the cupcake doesn't quite rise, if you follow.

Though I prefer to see the cup as half-full, not half-empty.

Anyway, the cup's shape was amazingly breast-like, though

completely fake, which made it perfect, so I told her to add it to my bag without really checking the price. And when I looked at the receipt, it was too late.

But I have a solution.

I'm putting it in my will.

There's financial planning for the future.

Heirloom underwires.

Mother Mary and the Terrorists

||||||||||||||||||||||||||||||||||||||||||||||||||

By Lisa

They say that the past isn't even past, and that's always true when Mother Mary is around.

It all begins with a call from Brother Frank. "I got bad news," he says. "We're bastards."

"Wha—?"

"Well, we went to get Mom's driver's license renewed."

So far, I'm following. Mother Mary doesn't drive, but she carries an ID card issued by the Florida DMV. Her last ID card expired, which I found out on her last visit after I tried to put her on a plane back to Miami. They wouldn't let her fly until they patted her down, which she enjoyed way too much.

"The DMV says we can't renew her ID card without her marriage certificate."

"Why?"

"Because she's a woman who's using her married name."

"So what?" I'm trying to understand. I don't see what a driver's license has to do with a marriage certificate, especially at this point in my mother's life. My father passed away in 2002, and my parents have been divorced forever. They were married in 1950, a time when people balanced spinning plates on TV. Now *that's* entertainment.

"It's a new law, since September 11."

In the background, I hear my mother yelling, "Those terrorists, they should be ashamed of themselves!"

I nod in approval. That someone should be ashamed of themselves is one of the worst things she says. And when she's really mad, she'll throw her shoe at them and shout, "Out of my sight!" I fear for the terrorists if they ever meet Mother Mary. She'll order them out of her sight and throw her shoe. She always hits her target. There are missile launchers with less accuracy.

I can't believe what I'm hearing. "Frank, can this be true?"

"Yes. We were in line behind a ninety-two-year-old woman whose husband had been dead for fifty years, and they wouldn't give her an ID card. She had taken two buses to get there, so we gave her a ride home. She said it was a *mikveh*."

"You mean a *mitzvah,* which is a good deed."

"What's a *mikveh?*"

"It's a ritual bath. Forget it. Tell the story."

"So we called the hall of records back home, and they can't find her marriage certificate anywhere."

"Do the records go back that far?"

"Yes, but the certificate is lost. Or it never existed."

I blink. "It has to exist. They got married."

"Yeah, but there's no proof."

Behind him, my mother's yelling, "It's all because of the terrorists!"

I let it go. "So what now?"

"She can't visit you until we straighten this out."

Which would be the good news.

Just kidding.

I ask, "What about a passport?"

"She needs the ID card. She's gonna show a passport to write a check? And we're illegitimate."

"Does it matter?" I wonder aloud. In the olden days, they used to call it being *born out of wedlock.* I never liked the word *wedlock,* though its faintly incarcerated air fit my marital history to a T.

"I don't think it matters. Everybody's illegitimate, these days. I feel cool."

I smile. "I know, right? We're like Brad Pitt and Angelina Jolie's twins."

"I'll be the girl."

I laugh. "Okay, I'll be the boy."

Mother Mary shouts, "Bastards!"

But I don't ask which ones she means.

Twit-Willow

|||||||||||||||||||||||||||||||||||||||||||||||||||

By Francesca

My girlfriend recently took me to a barbecue with the hopes of setting me up with the host. He turned out to be a sweet guy, a great cook, and we talked all night. So I was disappointed when he didn't get my phone number. He didn't even ask for my email.

However, he did start following me on Twitter.

The next day, there was a tweet for me reading: "Nice meeting you last night. I'm checking you out 140 characters at a time ;)"

I knew he was kidding, but all I could think was, *oh no.*

Are we doing this now? Do we really want to make Twitter the new frontier of having to be charming and attractive?

Demi Moore may have the time and the body to tweet bikini-clad self-portraits, but she's a freak of nature. I am a mere mortal.

Admittedly, I learned to flirt on AOL Instant Messenger, and I've been told I write good text messages, but this social media boom is expanding faster than my learning curve. Simply being born after 1980 no longer confers sufficient expertise.

I only recently opened a Twitter account, and right now, it's about the least sexy thing ever. I mostly tweet links to articles on animal rights, jokes about pop culture and celebrities, and pictures of my dog.

Are you turned on yet?

I also use Twitter for communal TV viewing. I live alone, so sometimes when I'm watching a particular show, I'll go on Twitter and search for other people watching the same thing at the same moment. I goof on dumb reality shows and watch Philly sports events with the greatest/angriest fans on Earth.

So essentially, my Twitter account is a web incarnation of me on the couch in fleece pants.

Not exactly first date attire.

Even if I took the lead pursuing someone on Twitter, it's an awkward medium for romance.

To "follow" a crush sounds like stalking him.

Which doesn't work, by the way. I "followed" this one hot senior guy for most of tenth grade, and all I got to do was his French homework.

Facebook is stressful enough. How do I make a profile that is friendly to friends, professional to professionals, and attractive to potential mates?

I'm onto the code words. For instance, if someone lists "working out" as their interest, activity, or one of their "likes," this is code for "I look good naked." No one "likes" working out. We like how we look after we work out. Or more relevantly, we like how other people look after they work out.

And the pictures on Facebook have gotten out of control. Initially, I wouldn't untag anything because it seemed too vain. But now that there are three million pictures of everyone, I've become more judicious, culling the unfortunate ones where I look too nose-y.

Trust me, with all that Italian spaghetti sauce in my blood, certain angles can get really nose-y.

Speaking of nosy, the Internet begs you to dig up the dirt on someone. Between Facebook pics, Twitter feeds, and good old-fashioned Google search, my friends and I can normally find a guy's graduation honors, employment history, ex-girlfriend, and at least one shirtless beach picture, all before the first date.

Is that a good thing?

Not when I realize he can do it to me, too.

My mom thinks all this Internet stuff is a generational thing, but if that were true, I'd be better at it.

I told my best friend about Twitter guy, and she offered a theory that every guy has his own preferred technology for connecting with a girl. I should mention that my friend is also drop-dead gorgeous, so she's had a lot of unsolicited experience.

She explained, "For example, Sam always used BlackBerry Messenger, and Topher would only text me, but Alejandro would actually call. I think that was a European thing."

After rattling off a few more names from a few more continents, she concluded that the medium says more about the guy's individual personality than anything else.

Later that week, I was still wondering how to proceed with my Twitterific flirting when I received a letter in the mail. It was from a guy I'd met a few weeks ago, before he had to go back to grad school in England. The letter was several pages long, thoughtfully phrased, beautifully written, and at the end, he politely asked me, if I wouldn't mind the extra postage, would I write him back?

I'm buying stamps tomorrow.

Grainy

||||||||||||||||||||||||||||||||||||||||||||||||||||

By Lisa

The great thing about being an empty nester is that you can eat anything you want, anytime. You know what the worst thing is?

That you can eat anything you want, anytime.

We begin when I drive Daughter Francesca to New York, because they don't allow dogs on the train, even in a carrier. It bugs me that Amtrak doesn't allow dogs, though they're allowed on airplanes. Especially since a train ticket costs only a billion dollars less than a plane ticket, and neither runs on time.

But that isn't the point.

The point is that I grab a quick lunch with Francesca in New York, and we go to our favorite Italian restaurant, where I take a chance on ordering something new. This is something I never do. I like to go to the same places and eat the same things, as you will see, but in this case I make an exception and order the farro.

The what?

I didn't know what it was either, but it came with tomatoes, cheese, and olive oil, which sounded like pizza, and pizza is so great that even things that sound like pizza are usually great. So they bring me a bowl of farro.

I taste it, and my life changes.

I love it. It's nutty and chewy and great, and I eat the whole bowl. I give Francesca a taste, but I refuse to share more. I hate to share in restaurants. I guard my plate like a wolf.

Or a corgi.

We leave the restaurant and I go on the Internet, where I learn that farro is actually an ancient grain, grown near Rome, in the province of Abruzzo, which happens to be where Mother Mary's parents grew up. The motto of Abruzzo is strong and gentle.

Her motto is strong and violent.

I also learn online that farro isn't emmer or spelt, but you could have fooled me, because I never heard any of these words.

But anyway, I go to the grocery store and buy three small bags of farro. Then I hurry home, soak half a bag for fifteen minutes, boil it for fifteen more, then add tomatoes, cheese, and olive oil. And devour.

I'm in food heaven.

I read the Nutrition Facts, and am happy to see that only 15 of the 170 calories are from fat, and farro is so filling that I'm not hungry all day or night, so I hardly snack at all. I try it with cheese and artichokes, then asparagus and all kinds of different veggies, and I love it so much I eat it for lunch and dinner.

Every day, for the next ten days.

I become Queen of Farro.

Or better yet, Pharaoh of Farro.

Ten pounds later, I'm starting to wonder. Francesca comes home for a visit, and I make her a bowl. "Delicious, right?" I ask her.

"Awesome."

"I gained weight, but I never snack anymore. I don't understand. Do you?"

"Maybe. Did you see this?" Francesca shows me the Nutrition Facts. "One serving is 36 grams of carbs."

"I know, but it's only 170 calories."

"Okay, but did you read the serving size?"

"No," I admit. "Most serving sizes are like two a bag, right?"

"Yes, but this one says ten. There are *ten* servings in one bag." Francesca gestures to our bowls, which are full. "This meal is probably five servings a piece. At 36 grams of carbs a serving."

I feel dizzy. I can't multiply that fast.

"In other words, your meal is 180 grams of carbs."

I blink.

"And if you eat it twice a day, that's 360 grams of carbs a day."

For a second, I can't speak. I know this can't be good. A low-carb diet like South Beach is 20 grams of carbs a day, but that's crazy. We go online, where we learn that the average female, if she's not dieting, should consume 180 to 230 grams of carbs a day.

Uh oh.

I can't subtract that fast, either. But I'm getting the gist.

360 grams of carbs minus 230 grams of carbs equals my jeans don't fit.

In Which We Lose Angie, and Nothing's Funny

||||||||||||||||||||||||||||||||||||||||||||||||||||

By Lisa

Today I have sad news to report.

No joke.

Our older golden retriever, Angie, passed away. I've been putting off telling you, because I've been putting off telling me.

The good news is that she was healthy all of her long life, then she got cancer. The bad news is, though she fought it, she didn't win.

And we lost.

You might remember Angie as the Zen golden, the un-squeaky wheel who was soft and fluffy, with a coat the hue of creamery butter. If you remember the stories about her from the earlier books, she was the one who helped me figure out why my dishes were cloudy. Until we heard from plumbers that what she and I figured out was impossible, pipe-wise.

Still, what can you expect from a dog, much less a woman?

After the diagnosis, Francesca came home and we took Angie to chemo for weeks, trying to save her life. She cooper-ated, too, trying to hang in there, and in the end, we were all sleeping on the floor together, day and night, until one of us needed to rest, forever.

What's interesting now, a few months later, is how this has affected the other dogs, especially Penny. You may remember that Penny is my other, and last, golden. They say that a dog is man's best friend, and that's true. But it turns out that dogs have best friends, too.

Penny's best friend was Angie.

They played and hung out together, every minute. They usually rested side-by-side, their postures mirror images; in fact, they were half-sisters, having the same father. The only difference between them was that Angie liked to sleep with her ball in her mouth. Evidently, dogs need pacifiers, too.

Our Angie

And though Angie was quiet and Penny rambunctious, to-gether they seemed to make halves of the same doggie whole.

Their favorite game was fetch, and Angie loved her red Kong ball, pockmarked with teeth. When we threw it for her, Penny would run to chase it down and always reached it first. We'd have to load the dice by throwing the ball closer to Angie, or even holding Penny back to give Angie a head start. Truth was, we did that more for us than for her. Angie wasn't the competitive type. She just was happy to run around in the sun with her bestie, collecting a lot of love, if not beating anybody to a ball.

There might be a lesson in that, but I have yet to learn it.

And now that Angie is gone, Penny, the dog we thought was

Best friends

Penny, alone

noisy and not at all sensitive, has changed. Specifically, Penny won't come out of the coat closet.

Again, no joke.

Since Angie's death, Penny has spent much of her day sleeping in the coat closet, which is something she has never done before. None of my dogs has. They're all at my feet, on my lap, or standing in front of the television while I try to change the channel with the remote.

I encourage Penny to come out and play fetch, and she rises to the occasion, cantering toward me with the ball, but it isn't the same. You would think she'd revel in always getting the ball and never having to share, but that isn't the case. Instead, she lies down after a time, tired sooner than she used to be, and today I realized that Penny was never trying to beat Angie to the ball.

She was showing off for her.

And now, her audience is gone.

The truth is, I'm getting more and more used to losing things I love. As are we all, as we get older.

That is, if we're lucky.

If we're not the ones getting lost.

And I don't think we get past any of these losses, whether they're dogs or people. We just tuck a little ache into a heart that gets softer and warmer with time, like dough kneaded by skilled and loving hands.

Penny won't get over Angie, and neither will Francesca or I.

We're not meant to.

We'll just carry her around inside us, and she'll be a dog that reminds us of just how human we really are.

Thank you, Angie.

We love you.

Banana Fanna Fo

||||||||||||||||||||||||||||||||||||||||||||||||||

By Lisa

I just found out that Mother Mary has been living under an alias.

You would think that I'd know my mother's real name. After all, she's 86, I'm 55, and it's the kind of thing that's generally well-established by now. But Mother Mary is full of mysteries.

Let me explain.

You may recall that I took her back to the airport after her last visit, and she almost wasn't allowed to board the plane to Miami, because her ID card had expired. The airline let her fly only because she was carrying her social security card. Of course, you could have guessed that Mother Mary carries her social security card. She also carries her voter registration card and a photo of Tom Selleck that she claims came with her wallet, but I don't believe her.

I suspect she just likes Tom Selleck.

Wallets haven't come with photos since the days of Troy Donahue. Photos don't even come with photos anymore. All the photos are in the cell phones, guaranteeing that the moments of our lives will last as long as a SIM card.

To continue the story, Brother Frank took her to the DMV for a new ID card, but they wouldn't renew her card because her last name, which is Scottoline, was different than the one on her birth certificate, which is Lopo. She had to go home and obtain her marriage and divorce certificates from when she married and divorced my father, and she also had to get the marriage and divorce certificates of the guy she married and divorced before my father, since she's divorced twice, in the manner of all Scottoline women, who need a couple of tries to get something right and often never do.

So she obtained the necessary documents and they went back to the DMV, where they waited in line for three hours, during which Brother Frank tells me that Mother Mary morphed into Line Police. He didn't need to elaborate; I've waited in plenty of lines with Mother Mary, and I know the drill. She watches everything and everybody in the line.

She makes the average hawk look asleep at the switch.

Mother Mary makes sure that nobody is butting in, holding a place for someone else, or taking too long at the counter. All such infractions are met with eye-rolling, theatrical sighing, or a well-timed "oh, come on!" And if the line shifts forward but the person in front of her doesn't move instantly, she'll lean over, wave him ahead, and say, "*Go.*"

Her finest moment arises when she spots the person who Just Has A Question.

You've seen this person.

He acts agitated when he bypasses the line and goes straight to the counter, as if his question was roiling his very soul. Most people ignore the person who Just Has A Question. Not Mother Mary. I've seen her stop the person who Just Has A Question and tell him he can take his question to the back of the line where it belongs.

And once, she said to him, "I just have a question, too. Why are you butting in line?"

To return to the story, she finally gets to the DMV counter, and the clerk is about to issue her a new ID card when he notices something. Mother Mary's birth certificate doesn't read Mary Lopo, but Maria Lopo.

"So what?" Mother Mary asked him, and me, later, when she tells me the story.

"Your name isn't Mary?" I'm dumbfounded. "All my life, you told me your name was Mary."

"It is. Maria is Mary in Italian."

"But this isn't Italy, Mom. Mary and Maria are two different names. I thought your name was Mary, but it's Maria. How did I not know this?"

"They're not different names."

"Yes, they are. That's why the man couldn't give you an ID card that says Mary."

"So now I got an ID card that says Maria Scottoline, but it doesn't match my bills, my credit cards, my social security card, or my deed."

"Your name really isn't Mary?" I ask, still flabbergasted. Twenty years ago, I named my first fictional character, Mary DiNunzio, after her. And for years, I've been calling her Mother Mary. But she isn't Mother Mary. She's Mother Maria.

She keeps talking away.

But I don't listen. I don't understand at all.

I'm the person who Just Has A Question.

Mousetrap

|||||||||||||||||||||||||||||||||||||||||||||||||

By Francesca

I try not to be squeamish. I was raised by a strong woman, and I'm working on becoming one myself. So the first time I saw a mouse in my kitchen, I kept an eye on it as it ran into a crevice beside my radiator pipe, quickly retrieved some steel wool, and calmly plugged the hole.

Problem solved.

For the night.

The next day, I was sitting writing at the table, when I saw something dash across the floor. I tip-toed over and peered underneath the dishwasher, but just as I caught sight of the twitching, whiskered nose, a second mouse emerged from beneath the oven and joined his friend under the washer.

I'm not afraid of one little mouse. Two mice is a different story.

I called my mom.

"Call your super," she said.

"I feel bad bothering him." I hate to bother people. But I love to bother my mother.

"Don't feel bad, honey. It's his job. And I can't really do anything to help from here."

Just letting me bother her is a help, but practically speaking, I see her point.

An hour later, my super, Ervin, arrived. He's a lovable lug with an Eastern European accent. He said, "I'm surprise you have mouse problem with dog."

I looked over at Pip snoozing on the couch; he hadn't lifted his head since my super came in.

Some surprise.

Ervin helped me pull out the oven and the dishwasher, where we discovered holes in the wall behind both appliances.

This is what counts as "newly renovated" in your first apartment.

After we plugged the holes, Ervin started to unpeel what looked like a giant sticker. "Glue trap. Mouse walk on glue, it stick. If one stick, it gonna make noise. Don't be scared. Call me, I come get it."

"That sounds sad."

He shrugged. "You can try get human traps."

He means *humane*.

"Do they work?"

"No."

I thanked him and said goodbye. But I did feel sorry about the cruelty of a glue trap. So I went out and bought the old-fashioned wooden traps, and I even found some humane traps. I set both, so the mice could choose their fate.

This mitigated my guilt, but I still hated having traps, period. Pip is unfazed by rodent activity but highly alert to peanut butter activity, so he was whining behind the baby gate I'd put up to bar him from the booby-trapped kitchen.

I couldn't just sit and wait. My apartment was clean, but I started cleaning anyway, and the more I cleaned, the more convinced I became that everything was dirty. Every place was a new place touched by mouse feet.

My neighbor told me that mice hate the smell of Irish Spring soap, so I bought three bars, peeled them with my vegetable peeler, and sprinkled the soap shavings all over my bedroom, at the back of my drawers, around the laundry bin, in the corners of my closet.

It smelled like a teenage boy exploded in my bedroom.

Then a friend on Facebook told me that mice hate the smell of crushed mint, so I bought fresh mint and made a mint moat around my bed. Within hours, it had wilted and dried out, so it looked like I was composting on my bedroom floor.

Then I read online that you must use 100 percent oil of peppermint. It said to apply it with a cotton ball. In retrospect, this direction probably indicated that I should use it sparingly, but I got carried away. When I was finished, my bedroom smelled like a candy-cane factory.

God knows if it's keeping the mice out, but at least my sinuses are clear.

That night, I tried to go to sleep in my Irish peppermint wonderland, but at every tiny sound, my body would go rigid, my mind hyper-alert, waiting for proof of mice. So despite the October chill, I turned on my rattling air conditioner, shoved cotton in my ears, and pulled a pillow over my head. Finally, I fell asleep and dreamt of a handsome Irish lad working in Santa's workshop.

Later, I awoke to a clicking sound. I reached for my glasses on the nightstand and slowly raised them to my face.

My worst nightmare was brought into focus:

A mouse, chomping on my baseboard.

It's *on*.

Pilgrim's Progress

|||||||||||||||||||||||||||||||||||||||||||||||||||

By Lisa

There is such a thing as too much progress. The proof is what happened to me the other day at the airport.

Before boarding, I make a quick trip to the ladies' room. Every woman of a certain age knows what I'm talking about. Whether we need to or not, we're going to the bathroom, just in case we need to in the foreseeable future, which is defined as the next fifteen minutes.

I'm talking about the preemptive pee.

This is similar to our equally adorable habit of carrying a water bottle everywhere, because it's important to stay hydrated at all times. It goes without saying that the water bottle and the preemptive pee are related, but that's not the point herein.

The point is that the ladies' bathroom is now fully automatic, which is a sure sign of progress. The world has gotten so damn smart that the toilet knows when to flush, the soap knows when to squirt, the water knows when to turn on, and the paper towel knows when to dispense.

In theory.

I go into the stall and do my thing, but when I get up, the toilet doesn't flush. I sit up and down, twice, but it still doesn't flush. I wiggle my tush in front of the sensor and nothing happens.

Well, maybe the sensor covers its eyes or throws up, but the toilet still doesn't flush and I'm done exercising for the day.

I press the red button, then hit it with my hand. Still, nothing. You would think I'd give up, but I don't want to be the woman emerging from the stall with an unflushed toilet. Guaranteed I'll run into someone who either reads my books or, more likely, remembers me from French II in high school.

Bonjour!

And you know the first thing she'll tell everybody at the next reunion.

Scottoline is a pig.

So I sit in the stall, wishing for a toilet handle that worked the old-fashioned, mechanical way. In other words, always.

But no.

Because now we can make toilets that flush automatically, so we do, proving that not every improvement improves anything.

So I wait in the stall until the ladies' room is empty, then I slink out and make a beeline for the sink. These days, I wash my hands after the preemptive pee, now that there's something called H1N1, which is a virus disguised as a computer password.

I wave my hands under the automatic soap dispenser.

No soap.

I wave my hand under the dispenser again, but still no soap. I go to the second, third, and fourth dispensers, waving my hands back and forth, then up and down, then around and around. Still no soap, even after the hokey pokey.

Okay, fine, I figure I'll do without the soap and just rinse my hands. So I wave my hands under the faucet at the fourth sink, but no water.

You know where this is going.

I try the third and second faucets, moving back down the line of sinks, and I end up at the first faucet, where a tiny jet of water splashes into my hand. We used to have faucets that you twisted on and off, using an anachronistic device called a knob, but those worked too well and got replaced by progress.

Even so, the water I finally got isn't enough to fill a thimble and I'm committed to hand rinsing, so I wave my hands under the faucet, but my water ration has expired. I use the water from my water bottle.

Yay!

Then I wave my dripping hands in front of the automatic dispenser to get a paper towel.

No towels.

I go to the second and third dispensers, but still no towels. I engage in some creative profanity and remember with a stab of longing the ancient dispenser for paper towels, which had no sensors, moving parts, or computer chips. You would see the edge of the towel and simply pull it free.

It was all in the wrist.

But those dispensers have gone the way of typewriters.

Which is what we had before laptops that crash.

You Can't Touch This

||||||||||||||||||||||||||||||||||||||||||||||||||

By Lisa

Here's what happened to me, last weekend. I'd just finished the draft of my next book, which left me with nothing to do and a residual feeling that I should still be productive. I'd been working on the same book for a year, and even so, wasn't ready for it to end, even after I'd typed:

The End.

Please tell me this happens to you, no matter what you do. That once you've been working full-tilt, it's hard to bring it to an abrupt halt. It's not that those of us similarly afflicted are Type A, because we're too nice for that. I prefer to think of us as adorable cartoon characters like Wile E. Coyote, who keep running in the air after there's no more cliff.

Meep meep!

Either way, when I finally finished working, I noticed some scuffmarks on the walls of my entrance hall and I couldn't forget them. I kept looking at them, and though I wanted to relax, sitting down in my favorite chair to read a book, the scuffmarks stayed in the back of my mind. I remember when the back of my mind used to be occupied by men, but in recent years, they've have been replaced by carbohydrates.

And, now, scuffmarks.

Five scuffmarks in all, covering the wall in the entrance hall, and God knows how they got there. They bugged me, though I'd never noticed them before. It struck me that scuffmarks shouldn't be the first thing people see when they walk into my house, even though nobody is walking into my house.

And under the scuffmarks, I noticed a line of paw prints. You don't have to be a mystery writer to know how they got there. Little Tony, my Cavalier King Charles Spaniel who thinks he's Little Tony Soprano, protects me by resting his dirty mitts on the wall and barking at the window. And whenever I leave the house, Peach, my other Cavalier, body-slams the door.

Plus I detected a generalized griminess around the baseboards that I couldn't ignore. That would be from Ruby The Crazy Corgi, who rolls against the wall like a hotdog on a rotisserie.

I should have been picking up the nice thick book I'd wanted to read. It was going to be my reward for the nice thick book I'd just written.

That, and lots of carbohydrates.

But no, instead I went to the kitchen cabinet and grabbed the spray Fantastik and a roll of paper towels. I got busy cleaning the entrance hall and the baseboards, to no avail. The scuffmarks still looked grimy and dirty, and now, wet.

I realized that the entrance hall hadn't been painted in five years.

An hour later, I had a new plastic drop cloth on the floor, a girl-size roller dripping with fresh latex, and a slim paintbrush for getting in the comers. I started painting the entrance hall and blasted music on the iPod. I sang while I worked, and the dogs watched, all of us happy. I was happy because painting is more fun than cleaning, and the dogs were happy because they had a whole new wall to mess up.

I finished painting the entrance hall, and it looked so great and smelled fresh and new.

But then I noticed more scuffmarks in the family room.

And there were still songs left on the iPod.

So I got busy in the family room, which was the same color, called Beethoven. Though it was Sinatra on the iPod.

A few hours later, I had finished painting the family room, or at least as far up each wall I could reach, making do-it-yourself wainscoting. Also I didn't bother moving the pictures and painted around them, which saved a lot of time.

Still everything blended okay, and it all looked so terrific.

And since I had plenty of Tony Bennett left, I went on a scuff-mark hunt upstairs, where there was more Beethoven. I found a ton of scuffmarks in the second floor hallway, and I painted it through most of the night and the next day, after the dogs had fallen asleep and the iPod had segued into old MC Hammer.

Yes, I was Too Legit To Quit.

And by the end of the weekend, I had a freshly painted house.

And I knew I was Type A.

The End.

Security Complex

|||||||||||||||||||||||||||||||||||||||||||||||||

By Lisa

Most of the time I think I'm in sync with the rest of the world. And then there's the times when I'm not.

Security scanners.

I just watched the TV news, and everybody is outraged about the new body scanners and pat-downs as they go through airport security. I'm not criticizing those people, but I travel all the time and I don't feel that way at all.

On the contrary.

Scan me. Search me. Bend me over. Stick your finger in my ear. Do anything you absolutely have to do.

I'll get over it.

Here's what I won't get over:

Being dead.

Yes, I know, the body scanners are an invasion of privacy. Yes, I have gone through them at three airports so far. And yes, TSA guys have already seen my ten-year-old underwire and my saggy white Carter's, not to mention my butt mole.

And you know what?

I lived.

They may not have. At least, they have indigestion or nightmares, and I feel for them.

In fact, I'd like to bring a little sunshine into the life of those TSA types. All they get to do is look at driver's license photos all day long. Can you imagine how much that stinks, especially given how we all look on our driver's licenses?

So here's what I say: Check it out, TSA dude. Knock yourself out. If looking at my scanned body does it for you, you have bigger problems than terrorists.

I've also had the new and improved pat-down, and I'm a fan.

Er, I mean, I'm not opposed.

Was it intrusive? You bet. I've had dates that didn't get as far, and they'd bought me dinner. I felt embarrassed, giggly, and silly. How could I not? Someone I hardly know got to second base with me, in Terminal A. But you know how long it lasted?

Three minutes.

I forget, how long are you dead for?

Oh. Right.

Now, I'm betting that most of the people bothered by the security scanning are women, at least they were on the news. It makes sense to me. We're congenitally modest, and even if we're not, we tend to worry about someone running their fingertips over our muffintops.

I feel the same way. This would be a good time to let you know that I sucked in my stomach during my pat-down. I wanted my TSA date to think I was thin, even though she was a girl.

Old habits die hard.

The women on the TV news said that the pat-downs had no "dignity," but here's what I have to say to my sisters:

Remember when you gave birth? Remember when you were in labor? Remember when you were in the hospital gown, with your legs in the air? Plus you were fifty pounds heavier and retaining more water than most swimming pools?

You sweated, you cursed, you pushed, and you know what else happened. I know I wasn't the only new mom who left a present on the delivery table.

If you don't know what I mean, you're lucky. If you haven't yet given birth, you'll understand when you do. Recall that I warned you.

And you're welcome.

So anyway, here's why this matters.

If you were dignified before you gave birth, you cannot tell me that labor and delivery didn't cure you. Half the world saw you naked and as undignified as it gets. And oh yeah, another human being popped out of your body.

Yikes!

I never understand people who say that childbirth is beautiful. This would be another time I'm out of sync. Childbirth is not beautiful. Children are beautiful. Childbirth is disgusting. Anyone who says otherwise has never met a placenta.

I'm surprised ob-gyns don't have post-traumatic stress from seeing a few of those a day.

The only thing we can all agree on is that childbirth is a miracle, but that doesn't change my analysis. As miracles go, it's easily the most disgusting. For example, the parting of the Red Sea would be cool to see. Also the pulling a sword out of a stone. And one final miracle, like getting on a plane and getting off safely, all of us, forever.

That's the one I want to see.

Mousetrap Part II— This Time It's Personal

||||||||||||||||||||||||||||||||||||||||||||||||||||||

By Francesca

When we left off, a mouse had just woken me up with its noisy chewing. Didn't its mother teach it to chew with its mouth closed?

I guess it's hard to raise them right when they come in litters of twenty.

Unless you have a TLC reality show.

But where was I? Oh yes, terrified and appalled in my bed. At that moment it hit me that these hippy-dippy methods of rodent removal—the peppermint, the Irish spring, the "human" traps—were not cutting it. The mice had violated the sanctity of my bedroom, and something had to be done.

I called Ervin the Slavic Super right then. As it was the third time I'd called him that week, and seven o'clock in the morning, he was not pleased to hear from me.

"You got to use poison. I got seventy tenants, I don't want mice even more than you. Soon they think they can run over whole building."

"But the dog," I said. "I can't risk it."

Ervin assured me it could be put out of the dog's reach and accused me of worrying too much.

No such thing. Just ask my mother.

"Exterminator comes this Saturday, only day this month is coming." His Slavic accent took on a sterner tone: "Listen to me, let him do what he need to do."

I hung up the phone. I was still firm in my resolve that under no circumstances would I allow poison anywhere near my precious Pip. But I knew there was truth in what he was saying.

Pests don't respect pacifism.

So I compromised. I decided I'd let the exterminator put down poison, and as soon as the deed was done, I'd drive Pip home to my mother's to stay for a month. After that time, I'd take all the poison up, and my son—I mean, my dog—could return.

Seemed like a good plan, until Saturday rolled around. The exterminator was supposed to come between 8:00 A.M. and 11:00 A.M. I got up at 7:00 A.M. to pack so I'd be able to flee the toxic zone immediately.

By 4:00 P.M., still no exterminator.

I know when I'm being stood up.

Finally, I decide to buy my own darn d-CON. I leave a Post-it on my door with my phone number and run to the store.

Of course this is when he arrives.

I catch the guy just as he is getting on the elevator to leave. I nearly throw myself prostrate before him.

As soon as he's in the apartment, I can tell something is off about this guy. He's friendly and nice, but also jumpy, excitable, talking a mile a minute. His near-monologue went something like this:

"What do you do for a living? Writer? Cool, I also run a T-shirt business. Hey, what's your sign? Aquarius? Me too! I knew it. Bedroom this way? Sure smells minty in here. That perfume? Are you judgmental?"

Even amidst the hysteria, this last question throws me. "No."

"I didn't think so. Aquarius, we don't judge people, we're not superficial. Like, don't take this the wrong way, but you're beautiful. I saw that picture of you and your friend in the living room."

"Oh, thank you."

"But if someone saw you now, in your sweatpants, glasses on—they might think you're busted. But they're only looking on the outside."

Thank you?

Officially uncomfortable now, I walk out of my bedroom. But our game of twenty questions is not over.

"Do you smoke?"

"No. I used to want to sing opera, so smoking's never been my thing."

"Do you smoke weed?"

"No, never."

"Never?"

"Never."

He practically exploded. "You have to try it! I can get you some!"

"That's okay—"

"Don't be scared, if it's your first time, I won't smoke, I'll just watch you do it."

Oh, well in that case . . .

At this point, all I can think about is getting this guy out of my apartment. I manage to usher him out the door, and just when I'm wondering if there is a polite way to slam a door in someone's face, he spins around with another question.

"So you wanna hook up sometime?"

For the first time all day, he accurately read my facial expression and backpedaled. "Hey, don't take that the wrong way. I mean hook up, like, you know, as friends."

"Um . . ."

"No pressure. You wanna hook up, you call me." He wrote his name and number on my service receipt.

I took it, thanked him, and closed and locked the door as quickly as possible. I breathed a sigh of relief.

Francesca should have called Vivi.

At least one pest was removed.

Which is not to say I didn't take his number, I did put it in my phone.

He's currently in my contacts as "Creepy Exterminator."

This Old Homebody

By Lisa

I get my neighbors' mail all the time, and I never open it, even juicy stuff like bank statements or brokerage accounts. I respect my neighbors' privacy.

Also I can see through the envelope.

We begin with me mistakenly getting some of my neighbors' mail in my mailbox. Specifically, *This Old House* magazine. I flipped through the first few pages, then I got more interested than I'd expected, and you'll see why.

The magazine has articles about beaded wainscoting and vintage accents, as well as "how to give your laundry room a spa spirit."

I stopped, astounded. My laundry room has no spirit, spa or otherwise. My laundry room only has dirty clothes, piled on the floor. I eliminated hampers a long time ago. Now when I have to wash something, I just open the door to the laundry room and throw it on the floor.

Gravity is my hamper.

Back to the magazine, which showed a photo of a woman in a huge laundry room with white cabinets on all four sides, a sink under a pretty window, and marble counters on which to fold towels.

Girl paradise, right?

I couldn't believe this was a laundry room. I checked the caption to be sure, where I learned that the counters were quartzite. I have no idea what quartzite is, but it makes a counter and that alone has me beat. My laundry room has no counters. I fold my towels on top of the washing machine, near sticky blue pools of spilled Wisk.

The magazine even showed a library ladder in the laundry room. I don't even have a library ladder in my library. Okay, maybe I don't have a library, either. But I do have a dining room with bookshelves.

Also the laundry ladder was painted lavender. And the laundry room wallpaper was covered with painted lavender plants. And on the counter was a pot of fresh lavender.

We get it.

But that isn't even my point. My point is that as I kept reading, the magazine started showing photos of men fixing all the broken things in an old house. There was a tall man with silvery hair installing a new windowsill of cellular PVC, to replace a rotting one. And a stocky guy with a brushy mustache drilling upward into a ceiling beam. Then a red-haired landscape contractor bringing a lawn back to life, plus a smiling man with a screwdriver, above a caption that read MASTER CARPENTER.

My interest in the magazine was growing, but it wasn't about the PVC sills.

The magazine was morphing into a man catalog.

And I started thinking, maybe I should order me some Master Carpenter for Christmas.

In other words, *This Old House* got This Old House very interested.

There was a heavyset guy installing a base cabinet, above the caption GENERAL CONTRACTOR. A bald dude, the Plumbing and Heating Expert, fiddling with some red pipes. A younger guy with a caulking gun, whose caption read, HOST.

I didn't know what he was hosting, but I knew who was hostessing.

What's sexier than a man with a (caulking) gun?

You have to understand that these men wouldn't have turned heads if they were walking around the mall. But installing drywall, fixing pipes, and painting things?

They're Mr. Right.

And not because they're hot, but because they're actually doing something. And in the fantasy, they're doing something for me, which means I don't have to do it myself. Also that it would get done right.

They're Mr. Done Right.

Remember, I'm the freak who painted her entire first floor in two days, and it looks it. In fact, I learned from *This Old House* that those blobs of orange paint I left on the white ceiling are called bleed lines.

Except that my ceiling isn't bleeding, it's hemorrhaging.

Bottom line, I have to buy a replacement magazine for my neighbor.

And I'm subscribing to *This Old House*.

I hope it comes in a plain brown wrapper.

Little Dog, Big Pill

|||||||||||||||||||||||||||||||||||||||||||||||||||||

By Lisa

The night started out quietly, but it didn't end that way.

I was sitting across the family room from Penny, my old golden retriever, who'd just had the doggie equivalent of a total surgical makeover. She was lying on the couch, her head stuck in a plastic cone, because I had to fix all manner of old dog things that were happening to her.

That they sound like things that are happening to me is purely coincidental.

She was forming little fat deposits everywhere and they were starting to sag. I also have saggy little fat deposits. I call them breasts.

My other saggy fat deposits aren't little. I call them buttocks. Well, that's only what I call them in print.

Also, she had started to sprout brown warts on her face. Some were flat, and others protruded, like the one on her left eyelid. When I asked the vet what caused them, she answered, "They're skin tags and they come with age."

I blinked. I remembered that that was exactly what my dermatologist had said to me, when I showed him a new brown mole on my own eyelid. The left eyelid, same as Penny. He'd said it came with age and called it a skin tag, too, but I secretly wondered if that was just a nice way of saying it's an age spot.

Bottom line, Penny and I have age spots. Due to the fact that we have age.

Age, Spot, age!

Yes, I have an age spot on my eyelid, and you can imagine how fun that is when I'm trying to put on eye makeup. If I want to put on eyeliner, I draw a straight line until I come to the age spot, at which point I make a sharp right turn and go around it, like a jughandle off of Route 38 in Cherry Hill.

And imagine trying to put blue eyeshadow over a brown age spot. No amount of powder can hide the spot. Blue plus brown equals men turning their heads away in revulsion.

In other words, it's a good look, for a Cyclops.

Maybe I should buy a new color of eyeshadow, let's say, in brown. We could call it age-spot brown. Then all my age spots would be camouflaged, but it would look like someone smeared dirt on my lids.

Here's mud in your eye!

So I was looking at Penny and thinking these things when I realized that she needed her meds. I went into the kitchen, got her antibiotic, and hid it in some peanut butter. All the other dogs trotted after me, as they love peanut butter.

Also anytime I go into the kitchen at night, we're talking good news for dogs. I'm never going in for a snack of water, if you follow.

Carbs are always involved.

So guess what happened next?

I started to give Penny her pill, but Peach intercepted it and gulped down the peanut butter with the pill inside.

Uh oh.

Suddenly the night was no longer quiet. Peach is a tiny Cavalier King Charles Spaniel and she weighs 10 pounds. Penny weighs 80. I checked the medicine bottle and the label read CIPROFLOXACIN, 250 MG. You don't need to be Doctor Doolittle to know that it was too big a dose for Peach.

So I'm on the phone to the emergency vet, whom I have on speed dial, and they tell me that the dose may be toxic for Peach, so I have to call Poison Control.

"But I'm calling you," I say, into the cell phone. Meantime, I'm hurrying for my car keys with Peach. "I'm on my way."

"If you bring the dog here, you'll still have to call Poison Control."

"From your office?"

Little dog, big head

"Yes. And they'll tell you what to do."

I can't believe my ears and I'm jumping in the car. "So I call for the diagnosis and I treat her myself?" That's what I say, but I'm thinking: Really? Can I operate on her, too? And if I do your job, will you do mine? Because I got a novel that ain't gonna write itself.

So, absurdly enough, I call Poison Control from the car, at speed, and for sixty dollars charged to my VISA, a vet tells me that Ciprofloxacin isn't toxic in that dosage, but if I feed the dog a dairy product, it will prevent absorption of the drug.

Which is how Peach and I find ourselves parked at a convenience store, sharing a midnight pint of vanilla Haagen-Dazs.

Emergency carbs.

The Flying Scottolines Reach Out

||||||||||||||||||||||||||||||||||||||||||||||||||||

By Lisa

Cell phones are supposed to make communication easier, but it doesn't work that way for The Flying Scottolines.

We reach out and touch . . . trouble.

It begins when I pick up Mother Mary at the airport, or at least I'm supposed to. I'm there early, confounded by the hi-tech Arrivals screen. It's guaranteed that no Arrivals screen will give you a quick answer to when anyone is arriving. Why? Because as soon as you manage to locate the Departure City on the lists, the lists shifts upward. Your eye found Miami on the fifth line from the bottom, but as soon your gaze traveled across to Flight Status, you're in Glasgow.

In other words, once you find the Departure City, it departs.

Doubtless this is because the new technology receives new flight information in nanoseconds and transmits it in even less than that, so nobody can get a quick answer from an Arrivals screen, which is how you know it's working.

So already you understand my theme of technology not helping.

The Arrivals screen, as best as I can tell, is informing me that Mother Mary has arrived, or at least her plane has, but she's nowhere in sight. I pace and pace, and then I start calling her cell phone, but there's no answer. Half an hour goes by, and I call Brother Frank, back in Miami.

"I can't find her," I tell him.

He laughs, thinking I'm joking. "Very funny. I gotta go. It's a new job, and my boss is around."

"Frank, I'm not kidding." I know he has a new job, and I wouldn't bother him at it, not in this economy. Never mind that I used to call him at his old job all the time and tell him I didn't have her when I did, which is the kind of prank that The Flying Scottolines think is wildly funny. "I'm not kidding, Frank. I really don't have her."

"You're gonna get me fired," he says, and hangs up.

Long story short, I run back and forth, ask around, and finally go down to baggage claim, though she has no baggage. Actually, she *is* baggage.

Just kidding.

But there she is, out in front of the terminal. Mother Mary, all white hair and four feet eleven inches, standing outside the terminal at the curb. I run to the rescue. "Ma, what are you doing here?"

"The man brought me here."

"What man?"

"How the hell should I know?" Mother Mary isn't confused, she's angry.

"But I never pick you up here. Plus I called you on your cell. Why didn't you answer?"

"I had it turned off, for the plane. Now let's go."

So we do, because another problem with technology is that you have to turn it on all the time, and I hope they fix that soon.

And of course, the minute we get in the car, she wants to call Frank, to tell him not to worry. I know he's not worried, and I don't drive and talk on the phone if I can avoid it. But she's convinced that he's worried, and we can call from my car, hands-free. According to this technology, all I have do is to talk to my car and it listens, which would be great if it were fifty-five, single, and ran on testosterone.

So I hit speed dial, and in a few minutes, the call gets answered. "Hel-lo," someone says in an English accent. He sounds like Anthony Hopkins as Hannibal Lecter in *The Silence of the Lambs,* which doesn't surprise me. My brother always answers my calls as Hannibal Lecter and calls me Clarice, which is another thing that The Flying Scottolines think is wildly funny.

"Frank, Mom wants you to know she's fine."

"Pardon?" Hannibal says.

"I got Mom, and she's fine."

"So sorry, Frank isn't here."

"Frank, cut the dumb accent. I thought your boss was there. She wants to talk to you."

"Truly, Frank has stepped away. May I take a message?"

Which is when it hits me that this is the best Hannibal Lecter impression ever, and Frank's new company has offices in Britain.

And this is probably his boss.

So I did the mature thing. I panicked and hung up.

Which is yet another problem with technology.

That you can get your brother fired, hands-free.

Don't Look Now

|||||||||||||||||||||||||||||||||||||||||||||||||

By Lisa

Here's what just happened to me:

I couldn't turn around.

What am I talking about? Let me explain.

I was sitting at my kitchen island, writing on my laptop and watching the football game. The refrigerator was to my right, and an iced Diet Coke and a bag of tortilla chips were close at hand.

This is called a home office.

And the dogs were sleeping where they usually do, on round little beds behind me, like Muppets on tuffets. One of them made a funny sound, so I turned around to check on them.

Or tried to.

Because I couldn't turn around, not all the way.

And there was nothing wrong with my back, and I wasn't sick or anything. I just had to make an effort to turn all the way around.

What?

And this happened the other day too, when I was walking the dogs and heard a car coming down the road, so I turned around to see how close it was. But I couldn't see.

My nose was in the way.

I couldn't see behind me without turning my whole body. What's going on?

I went on the Internet and got the answer I feared.

I'm fifty-five.

I did a search, and there was article after article by doctors, physical therapists, and scientists, all saying the same thing. That women lose flexibility as they age.

Hmm.

I knew that, as an abstract matter, but I didn't think it meant I couldn't even turn the hell around.

I didn't even know which part of me had gotten inflexible. One medical article talked about how "women 50–71 years could expect problems with shoulder flexion, shoulder extension, shoulder transverse extension, hip flexion, and hip rotation."

I don't know what they're talking about, but it can't be good.

And I don't know whether it's shoulders or hips that are the problem when you can't turn around.

But in all the articles, the advice was the same. As one website said, "These data indicate that aging women can improve and/or maintain shoulder and hip range of motion through participation in regular exercise done three times per week."

First off, "aging women"? How dare you. Go to hell.

Second, always, with the exercise. I walk the dogs two miles a day, every day, and I ride a pony that's older than me. What else do you want?

Exercise was the wrong answer, to me.

It doesn't seem fair that you should have to do something just to stay the same. Here's my reasoning: I expect to exercise if I want to lose weight. That's a change in the status quo. I also expect to exercise if I want to get stronger. Also a change in the status quo. If I want to change something, I should have to do something extra.

But that's not this.

I don't want to change anything. All I want to do is turn around. And until today, I could turn around like a champ.

I needed a better answer. I went back online onto Google and plugged "I'm 55 and I can't turn around," but I learned nothing new except that Isaac Hayes wrote a song called "I Can't Turn Around." He was in his thirties at the time, so I guess he really didn't exercise.

Bottom line, I refuse to exercise just so I can turn around. So the answer is clear:

I'm going to stop turning around.

Then I started thinking.

Maybe it makes sense that as we get older, we can't turn around. Maybe as we go along in life, we're not supposed to be looking back.

This is especially true if you've lived my life, where I've made major mistakes, and I'm not even counting Thing One and Thing Two.

In other words, as we get older, don't look back.

Look forward.

Keep going.

Walking is fine.

Put your past in the rearview.

If it were so great, you wouldn't have left it behind.

See ya on the road.

Mousetrap Part III—
Modicum of Solace

||||||||||||||||||||||||||||||||||||||||||||||||||||

By Francesca

The week following my visit from Creepy Exterminator, I found myself back at my apartment without my best friend, my faithful spaniel, Pip, who was safely away from the mouse poison, staying with my mother.

Not that said spaniel did much to protect me from vermin or drug-fueled exterminators. Still, I missed him terribly. I was all alone.

With the mice.

I sat in the new quiet of my apartment, trying to work, but I was on edge. I caught myself listening, waiting for the suspicious rustling of a rodent, or worse, the sound of one of my not-so-humane traps going off, or the very worst, to see some poor poisoned mouse stumble out into the hall, foaming at the mouth, eyes wild and accusatory, shaking a tiny fist in my direction.

In my imagination, all mice die with drama fit for the stage.

Only a sense of guilt and revulsion could compel me to do what I did next; I decided to go to the gym. It seemed like a productive thing to do with all my nervous energy, and it would be good to get out of the house.

I arrived at the gym, buoyed by that smug sense of optimism that comes after I put on my sneakers but before I actually break a sweat. I was bounding up the steps to the second floor of cardio equipment, when I ran into my friend who works there as a trainer.

Before I could even say hello, she said, "You will not believe what I found."

She led me to one of the back offices and reached into the wastebasket. "I showed it to my manager, and she said to throw it away, but I folded it up in this napkin so I could get it again." She retrieved some wadded up paper. "Do you want to see it?"

"What is it?"

"Oh, sorry." She looked over her shoulder and lowered her voice. "It's a *bed bug*."

I gasped. Bed bugs, the modern plague of Manhattan! Nothing inspires more dread and horror in a city-dweller than these hideous little bugs. Infestation and its accompanying shame are contagious. I actually took a step away from her.

"Oh don't worry, I killed it first," she said with a little too much pride.

Well, I was curious; I had never seen one in real life. I peered into the tissue. It looked kind of like a tick, only uglier.

"I found it on the stretch mats."

Ew. "And your manager told you to just throw it away?"

"Yeah. But I had to tell you."

"Thanks, hon." I went to hug her but thought better of it—a pat on the arm would do. "Well, see ya!"

"You're leaving?"

I nodded and jogged out of there. Fitness is not worth the danger of an insect that sucks your blood while you sleep.

Beauty is skin deep. Bed bugs burrow under your skin.

Later on, back at the apartment, I got a little hungry, but the prospect of cooking was less appetizing with the memory of mouse droppings on my kitchen counter still fresh in my mind. I decided that without the dog to worry about, I should take my laptop and go camp out at a café, like writers do in the movies. It seemed more glamorous than my usual writing on the couch in stretch pants.

I arrived at a nearby coffee shop, appropriately in costume with my shoulder bag and plastic-rimmed glasses, feeling like a romantic comedy might just pop up around me at any moment. I nabbed the last free table and ordered a veggie wrap and an iced tea.

I was bending down to retrieve my laptop, when an enormous cockroach skittered past just inches from my foot.

I fled to the counter, where I told the waitress, discreetly and politely, that there was a roach now climbing on the wall, and if she wouldn't mind, would she please cancel my order?

Surprisingly, she was surprised.

"You don't want the wrap?" she asked in a French accent.

"No, sorry. I've lost my appetite."

"Because of the roach?"

No, because of the weather.

"Yes, because of the roach."

"But it is only in the main room, there aren't any in the kitchen where we make the food."

Of course, roaches wait to be seated. For filthy, prehistoric insects, they're impeccably well-mannered.

"Look, no hard feelings, but I don't want to eat with a roach on the wall."

She rolled her eyes and begrudgingly handed me my money. "You know, this . . ." she paused, presumably to translate the best euphemism, "this *problem,* this is so with all of New York."

No it isn't.

Not in my apartment.

I only have mice.

Accommodating

||||||||||||||||||||||||||||||||||||||||||||||

By Lisa

I am always amazed at the lengths people go to to accommo-
date their pets. Me, especially. Case in point, I own more baby
gates than Octo-Mom.

Why?

Four dogs and two cats equals five baby gates.

I'm accommogating.

Sorry.

To explain, all of the Scottoline pets get along, except at
mealtimes. They don't like to share their meals.

They get it from me.

So when I feed them, I put Ruby The Crazy Corgi and her
bowl in her cage, in protective custody. But Peach eyes Little
Tony warily as they eat, then starts growling and barking until
a dogfight breaks out. It's not as scary as it sounds, because
Cavaliers are small dogs, and their heart isn't in it, so she just
bitchslaps him.

Literally.

But still, it's unpleasant. And since I feed them while I'm
eating breakfast or dinner, I have to get up and down during
my meal, refereeing while my eggs get cold, which annoys me
no end. Not to mention that Penny, my sweet golden retriever,

gets so upset she won't even approach her own bowl. She ends up retreating to her closet, where she mourns Angie and the fun life they used to have, when there were no feisty Cavaliers and plenty of red balls.

Plus the cats, Mimi and Vivi, have their kibble and litter box in the bathroom, so the dogs have to be kept out of there, and you know why. Guaranteed that if you buy your dogs some pretentious gourmet kibble, they will always look forward to cat, goose, or deer poop. This would lead naturally to the question of who's dumber, the owner who buys the overpriced dog food or the dog who thinks poop is a side order.

To me, it's a toss-up.

So I need one baby gate to close off the bathroom, and another two to close off the second floor during the daytime. If I don't, the dogs go up to my bedroom in search of my underwear, which they bring downstairs and display to the UPS man, who pretends not to see it, and for that I am grateful.

So far, three baby gates.

And no babies in sight.

Also, finding the right gate is a science. I go through baby gates like a new mother, experimenting with expandable or not, plastic or wood, and high or low. High or low is the trickiest of these choices. I start with the high gate, which claims to open like a door, but the handle never works. I segue to the gate with the lower height, which is called a step-over gate, but that's a lie.

It's a trip-over gate.

At least ten times a day, when I'm going upstairs or to the bathroom, I'm tripping over the trip-over gate. And if I'm not tripping, I'm lifting my knees high enough to qualify as a drum major. I spend my days marching around my own house.

And I'm tired.

You would think it's trimming my thighs, but no such luck. At my age, knee replacements are likelier.

And three gates later, we're not even at mealtime, when I put Peach and Little Tony into the nook in the kitchen, close them in with a gate, then separate them from each other with another gate.

You counting?

There are five baby gates on my first floor, set up around my house like hurdles. If I want something upstairs, I think very hard about whether I can do without it. Do I really need those warmer socks? Do I need them enough to step over two gates, then trip on a third? Do I really want to run an obstacle course in my own house? Of course not. But then again, to state the obvious, it's not my house.

It's theirs.

I'm just the lady who buys them gates.

Home Team

||||||||||||||||||||||||||||||||||||||||||||||||||||

By Lisa

I just came back from a dog show, where I bought a planter, a quilt, a notepad, and a keychain, all bearing pictures of Cavalier King Charles Spaniels, like Little Tony and Peach. My new Cavalier booty will join my I ♥ MY GOLDEN RETRIEVER sweatshirt, a Welsh corgi button and needlepoint, and a CAT MOM T-shirt. Plus I own a cap with a picture of a pony that reads, THE BUCK STOPS HERE. And now I'm about to watch the Phillies and the Eagles games, wearing my Phillies sweatshirt and covered up by my Eagles blanket.

In other words, I'm a bumper sticker.

If I love it, I wear it.

And the question is, why?

By the way, my car wears no bumper sticker. It has better taste.

Why do I do this?

I'm obviously not the only one. I had to bid against a bunch of other middle-aged women for that Cavalier quilt. The fur and the estrogen were flying. It was a catfight, over dogs.

The women were already dressed in Cavalier shirts and sweaters. Odds are they had a ton of other Cavalier stuff at home, but they wanted more, and so did I.

Why?

What's even weirder is that my new Cavalier stuff bears pictures of other people's Cavaliers. They aren't even my dogs, but I wasn't leaving that show without a Cavalier mug, at least.

So what's the deal? I understand why we wear the team gear to go to the baseball, hockey, or football game. We're showing that we're all part of the same red, orange, or green tribe. We belong to the community, whatever it is, whether it's people who love Penn State or ferrets.

And for some reason, we feel the need to tell others the way we feel, about everything. It's like this essay, summarized in three words.

Which might be an improvement.

And our loyalty apparel extends beyond teams and pets. I've even seen people at my car dealership, buying clothes with the car's logo. Who is this for? To show the car some loyalty? And what's next? Maybe a flag, with a picture of the car.

You're in Volkswagen country.

And with the exception of the team apparel, it would be downright odd to wear some of the stuff I buy in public. Last year, I bought a T-shirt that says BOSS MARE, which I have yet to wear out of the house.

I'm single enough.

Evidently, we need to tell, seek out, and belong to a larger group of people who love the same thing. Even though we might not like the other people who love the same thing, especially considering that we have only one thing in common.

Take the Phillies.

As much as I love the Phillies, the odds are pretty great that there are one or two other Phillies fans whom I'd hate. They could be felons or just plain mean. In fact, mass murderers probably watch baseball in prison. I wouldn't share a table with them, so why share a wardrobe?

The question gets even harder as applied to me, because I never go to any games. I wear my team gear when I watch the game alone, in the house. No one sees me except for the dogs, who wish I wore my DOGS RULE shirt.

But the pony would object.

And the cats wouldn't care.

Yes, I dress in Phillies red for the games, even when there's nobody to share the team love. And I get happy when I see that sea of bright red on the TV screen, though I'm a woman, suited up on the couch. I'm on the home team, even at home.

I'm a team player, minus the team.

Go, me!

Please tell me I'm not the only person who does this. I found only one other person who does.

He's eight years old.

Running on Empty

|||||||||||||||||||||||||||||||||||||||||||||||||||

By Lisa

We all know that our hormone levels decline as we age, and I have a new idea for a hormone replacement.

Tequila.

Who needs estrogen, when they have Patron?

I'm no alcoholic, but it seems the better way to go. First, it tastes great with big flakes of salt, and how many other things taste great with big flakes of salt?

Okay, everything.

But here's another reason: If you drink enough, you'll forget you don't have hormones.

I say this because my doctor was considering hormone replacement therapy for me, then we found out that hormone replacement therapy can cause breast cancer, heart disease, and stroke.

By the way, don't take any medical advice from me. I'm just here to tell you that your declining hormone levels are no reason to do the freak.

In other words, you may have more whiskers than your cat, but tweezers are a girl's best friend.

And it's not only your estrogen that's leaking away, it's your testosterone, too. So not only are you less of a woman, you're less of a man.

Symmetry is always nice.

And think of the other advantages. Your libido decreases, which is a fancy way of saying that your sex drive goes into reverse.

Like you lost third and fourth gear. And forget overdrive.

Actually, your sex drive isn't even driving at all, anymore.

It gave up and took the bus.

Whether you're married or not, this is excellent news. Why? Because you have better things to do and you know it. Your closet floor is dusty, and your underwear drawers are a mess. Your checkbook needs balancing, and it's time to regrout your bathroom tile.

Get on it.

The bathroom, I mean.

Without testosterone, you'd rather repaint the hallway than have sex. And without estrogen, you'll stop crying about it.

Ta-da!

Feel better? Glad you're here?

And if you're not married, even better. Because I can tell you right now, from my own personal experience, that if you're a woman over fifty-five, your odds of attracting a mate are the only thing lower than your hormone levels.

That's why I'm trying to tell you about the tequila. Me, I'm dating José Cuervo. Every girl needs a Latin lover.

Of course, there are physiological changes that take place when you start running on empty, hormone-wise. For example, the vaginal walls get thinner.

Good news!

If you thought your vagina couldn't lose weight, you were wrong. Ain't it great? I hated having a fat vagina.

I went online to learn about other changes to expect as we age, and one webpage read: "The pubic muscles lose tone, and the vagina, uterus, or urinary bladder can fall out of position."

Well, there's a word to the wise. Watch out for falling bladders!

It's hard to visualize how this would happen, but I suppose you could be walking along and your bladder would just fall out, like a muffler.

Don't trip on it. Step over it, then pick it up, so you can take it to the shop.

The body shop.

After all, if they can replace knees, maybe they can replace bladders. Same thing, only different.

Other positives? You can save money on Tampax and wear a white bikini whenever you want.

Okay, only one of those things is true.

If you have a white bikini, you're Barbie.

Menopause Barbie.

And of course, other than tequila, there're lots of other changes you can make to your diet to counteract the loss of hormones. Flaxseed is yummy, if you like chewing ball bearings, and it will stick between your teeth despite electric toothbrush, dental floss, and blowtorch.

I myself have started drinking acai juice, and that's a revelation. Thick, oily, and purple, it tastes like motor oil. I know how to pronounce acai, because it's the sound you make when you hurl from drinking it.

There are other advantages to having no hormones but I forget them, which is another thing.

Um, where was I?

Control Issues

|||||||||||||||||||||||||||||||||||||||||||||||||||||

By Francesca

It's Sunday morning, and my first thought is about birth control.

No, it's not because I had some wild Saturday night. As usual, the only one to share my bed was my dog.

My sex life isn't exciting enough for regret.

But I am on The Pill. I was prescribed it as a young teen as a remedy for problematic ovarian cysts, and I've stayed on it as the last stop of many steps to prevent pregnancy.

The first being no boyfriend.

Now, don't get me wrong, I appreciate the virtue of playing hard-to-get.

But nothing plays hard-to-get like my birth control pills.

Even with a prescription, there are so many barriers to getting my hands on these pills. And it's not even a barrier method!

First, there's the pharmacy. I live across the street from a Duane Reade drugstore, which is basically true of every New Yorker.

There are more Duane Reades in this city than there are pigeons.

But recently, Duane Reade signed some exclusive deal with a particular drug company, and they stopped carrying the generic I've always taken. The pharmacist gave me a new one without even telling me. When I noted the change, he said:

"You might experience different side effects, but it's the same thing."

I may not have a medical degree—or whatever pharmacists have—but I'd argue that if it has different side effects, it is not the same thing.

So I made the trek to a far-less-common CVS, only to find the metal gate pulled down over the pharmacy at the back. I had to read the sign twice:

CLOSED ON SUNDAYS.

This CVS has to be the only establishment in all of Manhattan that is closed on Sundays. They don't call this "the city that never sleeps" for nothing—normally you can get anything, anytime, anywhere, with free delivery. I can deposit a check at the bank here on Sunday, but I can't fill a prescription?

This inconvenience wouldn't be so annoying if I didn't have to go through it every month. It drives me crazy that I can't get more than one pack of birth control pills at a time. If I pay extra, I can get two packs, but never more.

Why is The Pill treated like a controlled substance? It's not a narcotic. It's essentially hormone therapy. Kids are up to some crazy stuff these days, but I'm pretty sure recreational hormones will not catch on.

PMS is not a party drug. Ask anyone I've ever dated.

No woman in her right mind would take more than directed. If you abuse painkillers, you can get high and maybe even get on *Oprah*. If you abuse hormones, you'll simply abuse everyone around you.

I'm not asking for a handout; I'm willing to pay. My insurance doesn't cover my birth control prescription, and that's fine. Ironically, my insurance would cover the enormous medical expense of being pregnant, just not the minor expense of not getting pregnant, but fine. I'm letting it go. I'll pay. Just give me the darn pills!

Why do I have to check in with my pharmacist every month? Is it because my pharmacist cares about me so much? Because I'm pretty sure my pharmacist has called me "Francisco" the last five times I was there.

Why does the government make this so hard for women? They're considering legalizing marijuana, but I can't get my prescribed birth control? Shouldn't they be facilitating my responsible family planning? I think motherhood is one of the most important and difficult roles I will have in my lifetime. I intend to cherish and protect that time when it comes.

And let's face it: I'm too old for an unplanned pregnancy to launch a reality TV career. Twenty-four is eight years too late for MTV.

Is it this hard to get Viagra? Because as long as we're moralizing an individual's sexual health, I think Viagra prescriptions should only be able to be filled by the wives and girlfriends of the men who need it. Forget "Ask your doctor," how about "Ask your wife"? The decision should be mutual, at least.

I watch the commercials, and I see a woman enjoying a peaceful day gardening, until her husband interrupts her with some dumb innuendo like turning on the hose. Can't a woman pot in peace?

And worse, I've read that Viagra prescriptions can increase the chance of infidelity, because the male patients feel newly entitled to—ahem—test their equipment.

Case in point: my friend's eighty-five-year-old grandfather is currently dating a twenty-five-year-old woman.

That is drug abuse.

I thought the twilight years were a time for family, sage advice-giving, hobbies, relaxation—not sex.

That's what your twenties are for!

Just kidding.

Only men in their twenties have sex.

The real question is, what kind of a twenty-five-year-old woman wants to date an eighty-five-year-old man?

One that can't get ahold of her birth control pills.

My Daughter Moved Out, So Why Am I Still Lactating?

By Lisa

Everybody knows that pets can be like kids, but around the Scottoline house, things are getting a little extreme.

It all started when the weather turned cold, and I began to worry that Peach didn't have much fur, so I found myself putting a little maroon dog sweater on her, to keep her warm. Not that she was going out for a walk. I mean, for her to wear around the house.

Okay, so far.

I did this for one day, then two, then three, which was when it occurred to me that she might not like wearing the same thing for three days in a row, so I changed her and dressed her in a navy blue sweater.

Uh oh.

Also, it's a turtleneck, and when her head popped though the collar, first her cute little muzzle and then her curly reddish ears, it reminded me of when Daughter Francesca was little. And I stopped myself, because I realized something. I'm becoming one of those people who dress up their dogs.

And you know what?

I like it.

Still, it's strange that my dog is wearing a wool sweater and I have on a polyester fleece. What does it mean when your dog dresses better than you?

That she'll get a date sooner.

I never judged people who dress up their dogs. On the contrary, here's my general rule in life: If it makes you happy and it's low-carb, go for it.

After all, people who dress up their dogs are just having fun, and so are the dogs, so what's the harm?

Still, let's be real. I didn't criticize those people, but neither did I think I was one of them. I thought I loved my dogs as dogs, but the truth is my dogs have become my children.

At least I'm not lactating.

Yet.

In my own defense, let me say that this is all their fault. Why? Because they started it.

Most of the day, I work on my laptop at the kitchen island while they sleep away on their dog beds, at my feet. But as soon as the cell phone rings, Ruby The Crazy Corgi sounds the alarm, and Peach and Tony start running back and forth with Penny, barking and snapping at each other's tails. And likewise, every time I pick up the phone to call someone, the dogs start the noisiest game of chase ever.

Every mother will recognize this behavior.

When Daughter Francesca was little, she would start singing loudly when I got on the phone, and moms I know say their kids always acted up when they were on the phone.

And we got the message.

Hang up and love me.

I think the dogs are doing the same thing. And I'd stop treating them like kids, if they'd stop acting like them.

Funny, I've said before that motherhood has no expiration date, because I know that you never stop being a mother, even when your kids have grown up and moved out. But I didn't think that motherhood was transferable, in that if I couldn't mother my child, I'd start mothering small spaniels.

But I was wrong. It's Mothers Gone Wild, starring me.

I can't be the only one who makes motherly allowances for my furry kids, can I? For example, they get the best chair, while I get the ottoman. And I make sure I walk them every day, instead of doing an errand I need to get done. And the other day, I overcooked a chicken breast and gave them the best part.

I didn't eat the burned part, though. I threw it away.

I'm a mother, not a martyr.

I Refuse To Dress Up
For The Mall

|||||||||||||||||||||||||||||||||||||||||||||||||||||

By Lisa

This holiday I did a lot of my shopping online. It's easy, it's efficient, and it doesn't involve taking a shower. You need to dress up to go out shopping, and at the mall, it's practically prom.

So I stayed home and clicked to get gifts for Daughter Francesca, but this turned out to be a bad idea. Shopping online is like life. Few things are as advertised, and there's always an unwelcome surprise.

For example, let's start with something simple, like a book. I buy tons of books, plenty in bookstores, online, and electronically, too. I figure it's karmic; if I want people to buy my books, I have to buy other people's books, and we all need to read more, as literacy is essential for democracy. The more literate we are, the better leaders we elect.

Well, in theory.

But as Dr. Phil says, How's that working for ya?

Anyway, I'd heard that Mark Twain had just published his autobiography, so I bought it online. Yes, Mark Twain came out with his autobiography, even though he's dead. What an author!

I myself am planning to write my autobiography ten years after I'm dead, at which point I'll be starting a new thriller series, several romance novels, a graphic novel, and yet another hilariously funny book of essays.

I plan to be very productive, in death. It's only now that I'm too lazy to dress up for the mall.

But apparently Mark Twain wrote his autobiography and asked that it not be published until a hundred years after his death, which if you ask me, is taking a big chance. How did he know we'd care? At this point, how many English majors are left? I'd thought we were extinct.

But anyway, I bought it online for Francesca, sight unseen. I figured, how bad can it be? It's Mark Twain. So it came in the mail, and its quality isn't the problem.

It's the quantity.

When I opened the huge box, I learned that the book is almost two thousand pages.

Why does it matter?

Well, the paradox is that though I shopped online, I don't want Francesca to know I shopped online. It sounds like I didn't care enough about her to take a shower.

Busted.

Even though I'm sure she'd still want the book, I can't give it to her with a straight face, now that I know it's as thick as cinderblock. And I don't want her to feel as if she has to read the whole thing. I'm an English major, and I can tell you I'm not sure I'll read the whole thing.

Although I did read Keith Richards's autobiography, which weighed in at 700 pages. These people have a lot of life.

But I digress. My other online shopping surprise was a

custom T-shirt I bought for her, because I found this site where you could upload a photo and put it on a T-shirt.

Great idea, huh?

Also, in theory.

She loves her dog Pip, so I got his picture and went on the site, where it said you could place the photo in the middle of the shirt or on the pocket. But there was no pocket, which was confusing, and it looked odd in the middle, so I played it safe and put it over the mythical pocket.

And then the shirt came in the mail.

I held it up.

The picture was way too small to even see the dog, and he's placed on the left nipple. And, it's nipple-sized.

Uh oh.

How could I give this to my beloved daughter? Would she wear her dog on her nipple? And do I really want to draw mens' eyes to that general vicinity?

So I decided to package the T-shirt as a nightshirt for her to wear to bed, and wrap it with the Mark Twain autobiography, to put her to sleep.

Or to knock out any man who looks at her Pip.

(Or her Pipple.)

Mother Mary and The Christmas Standoff

|||||||||||||||||||||||||||||||||||||||||||||||||||||

By Lisa

When we last heard about Mother Mary, I was worried she wasn't using her oxygen, as the doctor ordered, and her nose was turning blue.

Well, we were on our way to a blue Christmas.

Because we stopped speaking to each other.

Here's what happened.

One day, I just noticed that since our conversation about the oxygen, Mother Mary hadn't called me. She usually calls every three days or so, just to say hi, but it had been about six days, and no word.

So I called her, wondering, but she didn't pick up. Still, I didn't suspect anything. It isn't unusual for her not to answer, because she naps at odd times during the day. In fact, she takes lots of naps. Because she doesn't have enough oxygen.

Because she doesn't listen to her doctor.

Grrr.

Anyway, a few more days went by, and one day, I realized she hadn't returned my call.

Hmmm.

You may think I'm slow on the uptake, and you would be right, but in my own defense, there's a reason it didn't dawn on me that I was getting The Silent Treatment. I never had before, as Mother Mary much prefers The Yelling Treatment. Or The Nagging Treatment. Or The World-Class Guilt Treatment.

But not talking? It's against our religion. We're women, so we never shut up.

Anyway, to stay on point, I didn't figure it out on my own. Brother Frank's birthday came up, so I gave him a call and he told me: "You're in big trouble. Mom's not talking to you."

"Really?" I couldn't believe it, and frankly, it got me angry. "She's mad because I told her to follow her doctor's orders?'

"Yes. She said you were fresh."

Hmph. I wasn't fresh, I was right. So I did the only logical thing. I folded my arms, figuratively speaking. "If she's not speaking to me, I'm not speaking to her either."

"Hooboy," my brother said.

Happy Birthday, Frank.

And so we were at a standoff. If she was boycotting me, I'd boycott her right back. Days went by. I thought about her a lot, worried about her more, and checked my phone for messages.

Mother Mary was standing her ground.

And then I realized, if I was facing Mother Mary in a stand-off, I was going to lose. Because I'd seen her anger segue into a grudge, which is a different thing altogether. You've heard that matter can be a gas, a liquid, or a solid, but there's a fourth state.

A grudge, as held by Mother Mary.

Her grudges are more solid than any concrete. Her grudges could build fallout shelters. Granite wishes it could be a Mother Mary grudge.

I can be stubborn, but I'm still the daughter. In other words, the apple doesn't fall from the tree, but the tree is still the tree, if you follow.

And an apple is no match for a tree.

Especially the Mother Mary Tree.

When the holidays came upon us, and I felt my grudge beginning to wobble. I was still mad, but I was more worried than mad, and if something happened to her while I was boycotting her, this apple would become applesauce.

The holidays are the time we're most grateful for our family, however angry they make us. Or however silly they are for not listening to their doctors.

Families need each other.

Like oxygen.

So I called. She picked up, and I said, "Merry Christmas, Ma."

And she said, "About damn time!"

"I'm sorry I was fresh."

"I made another doctor's appointment. And if he says I have to use my oxygen, I will."

Which is her way of saying I'm sorry.

So everything is going to be all right.

Busy Signal

|||||||||||||||||||||||||||||||||||||||||||||

By Lisa

Here's what we don't have anymore that we need, especially during the holiday season: A busy signal.

Do you remember the busy signal? It may still exist, for all I know, but I haven't heard one in ages. It was a horrible beeping noise that you got if you called somebody on the phone, but they were already on the phone talking to somebody else.

This was before voicemail. And before computers. Spanx hadn't yet been invented, and telephones were two empty cans on a cotton string.

Let's slow down and analyze the purpose of the busy signal.

Here's the idea behind it, which is now itself extinct: If you were doing something, you couldn't be doing something else at the same time.

Silly. Quaint. An antique idea. Of course, nowadays we know you can do plenty of things at once. Like driving, drinking coffee, texting, eating a take-out salad, and changing the radio station.

But back then, if you got a busy signal and you wanted to talk to someone, you would have to do something else that no one does nowadays:

You had to wait.

Wait.

And wait. Then try again, and wait some more.

I like opera, so let me remind you of a scene in Puccini's *Madama Butterfly*. It's the story of a woman who's waiting for her lover to come home, but he got married to someone else, unbeknownst to her. So she's sitting there, kneeling with their child, both with hands in their laps, waiting for him. The entire opera stops while we, the audience, wait with her, in real time. You actually feel her waiting, and if you want to feel waiting these days, you'll have to buy a ticket to *Madama Butterfly*. Because nowadays, that's the only place that anybody waits.

Nobody waits anymore, for anything. Waiting was rendered obsolete by multitasking. We do five things at once so nobody has to wait, and now we hate to wait. We're trained to hate to wait. We can't wait. We don't have time. And especially not during the holidays. There's no time.

Peace on Earth, but I gotta go.

I'm that way, now. I buy a gift and can't wait for the salesgirl to go find a box, which is another thing that doesn't exist anymore. You could spend a fortune on a cashmere sweater, and it's guaranteed they'll still ask you if you want a box.

Here's what I want to say: "No way! Why would I need a box, for a Christmas gift? Nah, I'll just take that cashmere sweater and shove it . . ."

Sorry.

So instead, I answer, "Yes, thanks, I need a box."

The salesgirl will say nothing, but merely blink.

And I will say, "You see, child, a box is a cardboard thing with a top and bottom. We used to have them in the old days, before menopause."

She will nod to humor me, then say she has to go find a box "in the back."

But I have no time to wait, so I'll take the lovely sweater in a paper bag and grumble. And my gift sweater will turn out as wrinkly as I am, teaching me a lesson.

We're all of us doing too many things at once, especially during the holiday season. So I say, take it slower. Wait for the box. And if they don't have one, go to gift wrap. Guaranteed, in gift wrap, you'll learn to wait.

But flip it.

Enjoy your wait. Breathe it in.

Still your head, and your heart.

This is the time of your life.

Think of it as your own personal busy signal.

And in your head, it will sound like opera.

'Twas The Night Before

By Lisa

For Christmas, I got broken pipes.

Again.

Let me explain.

Just before the holidays, I went down to the basement.

First mistake, right?

Going down to the basement is asking for trouble.

There was water all over the basement floor. It didn't take a plumber to figure out that one of the overhead pipes was leaking.

Correction. Actually, it did. It took four different workmen to figure out what was leaking, but I'm getting ahead of myself.

I called my plumbing and heating company, and they sent over a plumber, who said I needed a heating guy instead, and next a heating guy came over and said I needed a plumbing guy instead, and then a third guy came over who could do both and told me it would take four thousand dollars to fix my problem, which was a combination of plumbing and heating problems.

That's all I understood, as I stopped listening after the four-thousand-dollar part.

But it had to be fixed, so I said yes, and they put me "on the schedule."

This was two days before Christmas. I stayed home and

waited for the plumber/heater guy to come, though I had three zillion things to do, among them buying last-minute gifts and turkey for Christmas dinner. When no one showed up, I called the company, and they said I wasn't "on the schedule," after all.

Oops.

No problem, any other week but Christmas. I had no gifts and no turkey. Time was running out. The company said they'd send somebody as soon as possible, which was Christmas Eve day. This was a problem, because it was the last shopping day until you-know-what, and all I had for the holiday dinner was cereal. Also the tree had to be decorated, so never let it be said that I leave some things until the last minute.

Because I leave *everything* until the last minute.

Also, if you recall, my last Christmas Eve was spent with plumbers and heating guys. If it's a federal holiday, I'm spending it with plumbing and heating guys.

So I said to the company, no thanks, don't send the plumbers on Christmas Eve. Send the plumbers on Monday, after the weekend.

What could go wrong?

You'll see.

Francesca and I enjoyed Christmas Eve day, picked up our turkey and fixings, and stopped by the mall, where we were interviewed by a TV reporter as one of those crazy last-minute shoppers. I blamed it on Francesca. On camera. That's the kind of mother I am.

So we came home all happy, but as we were decorating the tree, we noticed it was getting cooler in the house. And long story short, on Christmas morning, we opened our presents in fifty-five-degree weather.

Inside.

Whatever had gone wrong in the basement had knocked out our heat, but no worries, we were warmed by tidings of comfort and joy.

Until the house temperature dipped to fifty-two.

Hmm.

We had put shopping ahead of heating, and now we're going to pay for it.

Still, no worries. We remained calm. We would tough it out for the weekend, then the plumber/heater guy would come on Monday.

But a snowstorm came instead.

And the plumber/heating guy couldn't.

So you know where this is going.

We have no heat, for five days now. Francesca keeps a fire burning in the fireplace in the family room, and I keep the hot chocolate coming. We sleep on couches, huddled with the dogs, in the flickering light of the fire.

So I asked her if we should have done the prudent thing and let the plumber come, instead of having Christmas Eve.

"Nah," she answered, with a smile.

Good girl.

Prepare for the Best

||||||||||||||||||||||||||||||||||||||||||||||

By Francesca

Recently, I met a boy. He's smart and cute and funny. And when I'm talking, he looks at me, *really* looks at me, and makes me forget what I'm saying. So you know what I told myself?

Don't get excited.

But I was. I could feel it fizzing inside of me like someone shaking up a soda can. Instead of enjoying it, the next thing I told myself was this:

Don't be stupid.

The butterflies in my stomach felt more like hornets, and I was just waiting to get stung.

When my girlfriends asked about this new guy, I heard my-self downplaying it, starting sentences with, "It will probably be nothing . . ." and just to be clear, "I'm not getting my hopes up or anything."

After listening to my litany of worst-case scenarios, my one friend said, "You know, you're allowed to be excited."

I am?

Oh, right, I am.

So why was I being so hard on myself?

We're often told that the problem with women is that we live in fairy tales—head in the clouds, nose in the air, dreaming of

Prince Charming while overcharging our credit accounts. The adjective *picky* is exclusive to children who won't eat and adult women.

But I have never identified with that, and the majority of women in my life don't fit that bill either.

In my experience, it's women who are the realists, the worriers.

How many real women do you know who are *too picky*? For every one I know, I can think of ten who are not picky enough, who are too quick to settle for a man who doesn't treat them right and too slow to get out of a relationship gone bad.

Common wisdom says: keep your expectations low, and you'll always be pleasantly surprised.

But at what cost? What does a life of low expectations feel like?

Surprisingly unpleasant.

We miss out on the giddy fun of fantasy and the adrenaline jolt of new possibilities.

I remember in high school when I could fixate on a random boy in class. My friends and I would discuss him endlessly and put his name into a game of MASH or Ouija board. I don't remember if I ever told the guy how I felt; that was beside the point. The dreaming was the fun part.

And no offense to high school boys, but most of the time, having the crush was better than having the boyfriend.

As adults, we don't often allow ourselves to get our hopes up about a new prospect, romantic or professional. In an attempt to guard against potential disappointment, we've made happiness the unexpected and pessimism the status quo.

And are we safer for it? Stronger? Braver?

Not really.

I'm starting to think that if you try to steel yourself against every blow, your armor just weighs you down.

And when does anticipating the worst slide into precipitating the worst?

If we expect little, we ask for little. We aren't as quick to notice when our low expectations have become simply low standards.

I'm not saying we should be reckless, but there is a difference between being grounded and being pessimistic. I think we should seize happiness whenever we can get it. It's our nourishment, our rocket fuel. It's worth the risk.

Joy matters.

It's not so much about trusting the world to take care of us, it's about trusting ourselves to push through anyway. We must have faith in our ability to bounce back from disappointment and failure.

Failure is an event, not a definition.

We can put it behind us and be open to the next person or opportunity that gets our blood pumping.

Disappointment does happen. But there's no need to roll out the red carpet for it.

So in 2011, I think we should give ourselves permission to fantasize, to get excited without apology. Let's go ahead and get our hopes up for a change.

Here, I'll start: I'm going on record saying I am excited about a boy. And if you see me sometime in the next year, and you ask about him, I'll tell you the unabashed truth. I can't promise it will be good news, but I can promise you that no matter what, I'll still be standing tall.

And so will you.

Because we can handle it when things go wrong.

So let's enjoy it, just in case they go right.

Join Me

||||||||||||||||||||||||||||||||||||||||||||||

By Lisa

I've said that I don't like the idea of New Year's resolutions. They're too negative. Why start out the year with a long list of things you do wrong?

Especially when you're so great.

How do I know you're great?

You're here, aren't you?

Bottom line, you and me, we're great already.

That's why I make unResolutions. In an unResolution, I resolve, in the new year, to keep doing something that I like about myself. For example, I like that I kiss my dogs on the lips. And I resolve to keep doing it.

Why?

It's fun, and it doesn't hurt anybody except my dogs, who are permanently scarred.

But they can't hire a lawyer, so no worries.

Now that we've established that I'm no fan of resolutions, you'll understand why I feel cranky at the people who pressure you into making them. There's even a website that will tell you to make a resolution and create a contract with yourself about it. You can choose from among the resolutions, which are "lose weight," "quit smoking," or "exercise regularly." Or you can even make a "custom goal."

You can guess my "custom goal."

I typed in, "marry George Clooney."

The way the website works is that if you don't keep your resolution, you break your contract with yourself. I don't know if you have to sue yourself or not, but this may be where my dogs come in. If you can sue yourself, they can sue me, and we're all in deep dog-doo.

The website also tells you to create a penalty so you don't break your resolution, i.e., it challenges you to "put your money where your mouth is." It says that you should set a dollar amount, whereby you pay money if you break your resolution.

Do you understand this? It means that you have to lose your own money if you decide to ditch George Clooney.

That's crazy. And if you ditch George Clooney, you not only lost your money, you lost your mind.

According to the website, exactly 52,283 people have already made contracts, for a total amount of $5,479,151.

Wow!

That's real dough. I'm pretty sure we could pay off the federal deficit with all the people who resolve they're going to start working out, but don't, like me. We'd have to pay off not only the gym membership we're not using, we'd have to pay the website, too. We can feel bad about ourselves—twice!

Happy New Year?

And if you're wondering what the website does with the money, it sends it to "a friend, a charity, or an AntiCharity, which is an organization you hate!"

Consider the first option: that it sends the money to your

friend. In my case, let's say I make a contract to lose weight and the beneficiary is my Best Friend Franca. Then, if my resolution is that I will lose weight, which is my forever-resolution from the days when I used to make resolutions, and I don't lose weight, Franca gets a hundred bucks.

Huh?

This means that Franca, my alleged best friend, would have to sit around and hope that I didn't lose weight. She'd cash in only if I fail. Is this the kind of behavior we want to encourage in our BFFs? On the contrary, that's the way to turn a friend into a frenemy.

Also Franca would never do it. She would tell me I didn't need to lose weight, no matter how chubby I was. In fact, she'd love me more, the more there was of me to love. That's why she's a true BFF and not a fake dumb website BFF.

And consider the penalty money going to charity. If I didn't lose weight and broke my contract with myself, my hundred bucks would go to an animal shelter. That's a win–win, to me. Dogs get rescued, and I get chocolate cake.

I guess that's why they came up with the AntiCharity idea, where the money goes to an organization you hate. Let's pick an organization that everyone hates, like the Ku Klux Klan. This way, if you don't lose weight, you're funding the KKK.

Ya happy yet?

Maybe I should start my own AntiCharity.

You can join.

We'll call it People Organized Against Resolutions.

That'll fix 'em.

Rewarding, or Why Free Is Dumber Than You Think

||||||||||||||||||||||||||||||||||||||||||||||||||

By Lisa

Here's what I'm telling you. Beware of "rewards points."

What?

Yes, that's right. I said it, and if you remember, it wasn't always thus. I used to be a big fan of rewards points.

Let's review.

I remember the day I found out that my credit card was accumulating rewards points, because I felt like I had won the lottery.

Okay, a really tiny lottery, but still, free is free, and I was excited. The way my credit card worked was that every time I used it, it accumulated points that enabled me to choose free stuff from a free catalog.

Wow!

I even wrote about how hard it was to pick stuff out of the free catalog, mainly because I was so dazzled by the free part that I thought I might faint.

I'm not cheap, but free has a unique power, no? I couldn't go wrong, if it didn't cost me anything.

Or so I thought.

And since then, I've been all over the rewards thing. I've even spread the word. Daughter Francesca is about to get a new credit card, and I've advised her to make sure she gets one with rewards.

Who doesn't want to be rewarded?

Lately, me.

I came to this epiphany with my new spice rack. I saw it in the free catalog, and I forget how many points it cost, because it all came down to the same thing:

It's FREE!

So I bought/ordered/willed it to exist in my house. And now, sitting atop my oven, is a too-cool-for-school spice rack from Dean & DeLuca. All of the spices are in glass test tubes with real corks, so they're visible from the side and have nice colors. But the spices are things like lavender and Tellicherry peppercorns.

Huh?

I have no idea when lavender became a spice, but it does look pretty in its purple test tube. Too pretty to use, and anyway, what would I put lavender on?

Marigolds?

The rack also includes imported spices, like Greek oregano and French tarragon. Thank God. You wouldn't want tarragon from anywhere else, would you? And I smelled the Greek oregano, which smells exactly like American oregano, which smells like a pizza parlor.

So maybe that, I'll use.

Or eat out of the jar.

But I've never used any of the spices in the rack, and the test tubes don't say when they expire, so the bottom line is, the

French tarragon should have stayed in Paris. It was a waste, even though it cost nothing.

Paradoxical, no?

The spice rack taught me that even though something is free, I might not want it. I don't need it. I'm not going to use it. If I had really wanted the spice rack, I would have bought it, and the fact that I didn't means I shouldn't have it in my house.

Even free.

That was my life lesson.

Let me interject to say that the problem may be endemic to spices. Even before the test-tube spice rack, I'd been known to buy spices that I'd never use. Mainly because I want to be the kind of person who cooks with green curry, I'd buy some and throw it out when it became a solid block of greenness. I'd make this same mistake around the holidays, when I'd pick up fresh jars of allspice, ground cloves, and cinnamon, which is the kind of thing I imagine the Cake Boss tosses into his shopping cart. But I never use it, and I'm no Cake Boss.

Cake is the boss of me.

Come to think of it, the real problem may be that I'm a stinky cook, as I barely use any spices at all, and in this regard, I'm my mother's daughter. There was no spice rack in our house growing up, and only four spices: dried oregano, garlic salt, onion salt, and salt.

Mother Mary cooked Italian, and salt.

We didn't even have pepper, because Mother Mary is enough pepper for anybody.

And to this day, when she visits me and makes meatballs or tomato sauce, we first make a trip to the grocery store to buy her salts, with their preservatives included, the faker the better.

And you know what?
Her food tastes delicious.
And I feel rewarded.
Almost free.

Can't Start A Fire Without A . . .

|||||||||||||||||||||||||||||||||||||||||||||||||

By Lisa

You may have heard that I'm single, and I like being single, because after two marriages and two divorces, I'm finally the boss of me.

What a great boss I am!

And what a great employee!

In both capacities, I'm easy and fun to work with. I never dock my pay and I always do my best. I give myself great performance reviews, and now I'm thinking about eliminating performance reviews altogether. Who's to stop me?

Nobody!

Yay!

And going along my merry single way, I've learned to do many of the tasks that Thing One and Thing Two used to do.

There weren't that many.

And to tell the truth, there was something that both Thing One and Thing Two could do very well.

Make a fire.

Whether it was in the fireplace or the grill, they were good at fire.

I'm not.

I try not to think that this is gender-related, but men have made fire since caveman days, while women stayed inside, swept the cave, and plotted divorce.

Anyway, since I've gotten single, I've cleaned gutters, taken out trash, painted walls and windowsills, and even hammered something.

I'm pretty sure I did that, once.

Or, again, to tell the truth, I've hired somebody to do all of the above. So I have all the same things I had before, except the fire part, which I have done without, to date.

But now, ages later, I'm missing fire.

Not the barbecue. I'm single enough without smelling like lighter fluid.

But I do miss a fire in the fireplace. I liked having a homey family hearth, even though I'm a family of one.

I count!

That's the trick to single living. Don't do less for yourself just because you're the only one around. Don't discount yourself. It's no way to live, with the idea that your wishes don't matter.

And this is true, whether you're married or not.

I think it happens a lot around the holidays. We go on discount, selling ourselves cheap, like a January white sale. It might happen because we do Norman Rockwell math, namely that ten people around the table = family.

But family can be you, alone.

After all, this is a country founded on the notion that one person matters. Think of one man, one vote. If you matter on Election Day, you matter the rest of the year. So make yourself a nice lasagna and pour yourself a glass of Chianti.

You get the leftovers, too.

Back to the story. I was missing a fire in the fireplace, but I'd never done it myself and I found it mystifying. Again, the caveman thing. Ooga booga. Fire is magic!

But I decided to give it a whirl. I remembered something about kindling, so I went outside and picked up sticks, then I remembered something about rolled up newspapers, so I did that, too. Next, I found some old logs and stacked them up in some sensible manner. And thanks to Bruce Springsteen, I knew I needed a spark.

Then I lit the mess.

Well.

You know the expression, where there's smoke, there's fire? It's not true.

I had smoke, but no fire. And furthermore, I had a family room full of thick gray clouds, smoke alarms blaring, dogs barking, cats scooting, then phones ringing, and burglar alarm people calling, which ended in me giving them my password.

Which is HELP!

I called Daughter Francesca and told her what happened, and she said: "I'll be home next week. I'll teach you how to make a fire. It can be done, and by a girl."

And one week later, she came home, piled the kindling, rolled the newspaper, stacked the logs, and made a perfect fire. The cats, dogs, and I stood in an awed and happy circle.

"How did you do that?" I asked.

"You gotta warm the chimney first. Hold the roll of newspaper up, like this." Francesca hoisted a flaming torch of newspaper, like the Statue of Liberty. "See? You can do this."

"Sure I can," I said, inspired.

I count!

I vote!

I'm American!

So I can be the Statue of Liberty.

She's a girl, too.

Cold Comfort

|||||||||||||||||||||||||||||||||||||||||||

By Francesca

It's cold in my apartment.

No seriously, it's really cold, way colder than whatever you just imagined.

Let me paint a picture. While I'm writing this, I'm bundled in three layers on top, a blanket on my lap, a hat, scarf, and fingerless gloves. I'm warming my hands by the glow of my laptop, like some sort of yuppie hobo.

Carrie didn't look like this on *Sex and the City*.

Why is it so hard to heat 400 square feet?

First off, the building's radiant heat doesn't kick in until the afternoon. I would complain about this, but I am so extraordinarily lucky to work at home every day, I accept the tradeoffs:

Cold mornings, and I can't steal toilet paper from myself. Sacrifices.

Also, my apartment is as drafty as a barn. Why? Well, all the windows in my "newly renovated apartment" have sunk in their frames, so that a tiny sliver at the top opens directly out to the air, even when the window is shut. I used my Can-Do attitude to assess the problem. I figured out that, to fix it, I'd have to push the top window all the way up and somehow hold it there with a one-handed Spidey-suction grip, then with my other hand, press the bottom windowpane back down, and finally turn the lock to hold everything in place.

Easy, right?

But the window is very tall, so I had to stand in the windowsill. I was pushing up on the top with my nose pressed against the icy-cold glass, when I looked out and down to the alley six stories below. It occurred to me that the only thing between me and those ant-sized pigeons was an already-malfunctioning window.

Can-Do attitudes go right out the window when you realize you Can-Die.

So now I pull the shades all the way up and embrace denial.

But I can't blame it all on the building, I'm partially responsible for the chill in the air. How?

I'm cheap.

I could get a space heater, but do you know how much energy that sucks up? I'd like to say I'm opposed on behalf of the environment, but I'm mainly an advocate for the environment of my bank account.

Numbers are dwindling. Extinction is a constant fear.

Did I say cheap? I meant I'm a conservationist.

Money is green, isn't it?

So I had an epiphany—put on another layer. Genius!

But I'd heard it somewhere before.

Oh right, Mom.

This fight was an old favorite when I was a kid. I used to always complain that it was too cold in the house.

I'd come downstairs for breakfast in my pajama pants and a T-shirt and announce, "It's freezing in here!"

"You're barefoot. It's too cold for bare feet," my mom would say.

"But I hate socks." I do, especially sleeping in them. They always come half-off in the middle of the night, and why? What kind of inferior clothing item falls off of you when you're lying still? Anyway, "Can't we just turn up the heat?"

"No. You aren't dressed warmly enough. It's winter."

"Outside, it's winter. Inside, it's home. Home is supposed to be comfy."

"I am comfy, wearing this sweater. Go upstairs and get one. And put on socks."

I'd pretend to cooperate, but later, I'd tiptoe over to the thermostat in my newly be-socked feet and try to kick it up a few degrees. But I never got away with it. My mom is positively reptilian in her sensitivity to heat, and within minutes she had it back down.

Why did I think I could fool the woman who has accurately guessed my temperature on every sick day since I was four years old?

If I accused her of stinginess, and I probably did, she'd tell me it wasn't about the money:

"You adapt to the world, the world does not adapt to you."

Well, it took me twenty-four years, but I finally got it.

So look Ma, more layers!

But she isn't here to see. That's the thing about moving out— your parents aren't around to enjoy the fruits of their nagging, and you don't get that hug or approving smile for a job well done. You have to be warmed by the knowledge of a lesson learned.

Cold comfort.

Lunatic

|||||||||||||||||||||||||||||||||||||||||||||||||||||

By Lisa

Great news! There's a new line of "toning" sportswear that loses weight for you. All you have to do is put it on. So go get some ice cream and make yourself a milkshake. Let's lose some weight!

Count me excited.

I knew this would happen, someday. It proves that America is the greatest country on Earth, making genuine scientific advances, one after the other.

Excuse me. Pass the chocolate cake.

If we can put a man on the moon, I knew it wouldn't be long until we did something that really mattered.

Because who wants men on the moon?

That's lunacy.

If you ask me, we need all the men we can get, down here. For a long time now, I've been noticing a general scarcity of men on the planet. Or at least in the tri-state area. Or perhaps only in my vicinity.

Or my house.

If not for the UPS guy, I'd never see leg hair.

I mean, somebody else's.

Thank God we've stopped sending men to the moon and we're now inventing clothes that lose weight for you.

Obviously, we do care about weightlessness. Only on Earth. Near our hips.

USA! USA! USA!

If you remember, it started a while ago, with the shoes that exercise your legs and butt for you. Maybe you read about them. They look like double-decker sneakers with extra padding in the heels, which is the special secret invention for weight loss. I got a pair when they came out and put them on lickety-split. Then I sat down and waited.

Wait, wait, wait.

But I lost no weight, weight, weight.

They didn't work. They must have been defective. But I didn't return them, because that would have involved getting out of my chair.

Sit, sit, sit.

Come to think of it, maybe these inventions began before weight-loss sneakers, as far back as weight-loss books. I bought a ton of them, then sat down and read them all, but they didn't work either.

Still, I never give up. I'm American, and when it comes to losing weight, I'll buy what it takes.

So now I'm pinning my hopes on clothes. If I just buy the right clothes, I feel sure I would lose weight. That's the thing about losing weight. They tell you that all you have to do is to diet and exercise, but that's not possible, as anybody who has tried it knows. There has to be a special secret thing you have to buy, that all the skinny/rich/Hollywood people know about.

Well, to be honest, I'm not sure who else knows it, maybe the people who got the good pair of weight-loss sneakers. Or maybe everybody but me.

I used to think they'd invent a weight-loss hat. Or maybe a wand that you could wave around. A weight-loss wand.

Bibbity bobbity, butt!

But today, I read in the paper about the toning tights, tank tops, shorts, and Capri pants that make you lose weight. They're black, which is a great start, if you ask me.

I'll be a stick of licorice in no time!

I went to the company website and clicked on body toning gear, where they explained that the special layering of fabric in the clothes increases muscle effort by 50 percent.

See? It's "special" fabric, that's why it works. You're probably wearing "normal" fabric.

Silly.

How can you expect to lose weight if you don't buy something special?

You need special layers to get rid of your layers.

The tank is $40, the pants are $55, and the shipping is $8. So let's do the math together. That's about a hundred bucks, and if you have three layers of fat around your waist, like some writers we know, then that's about thirty bucks a layer. I'd pay thirty bucks to get rid of one of my layers.

What an invention!

One online review of the clothes said that the special fabric increases "blood flow and oxygenation," which makes your muscles work more efficiently.

See, that's another problem. I have inefficient muscles. You might, too. But if we squeeze our slacker muscles into the special secret toning gear, we'll lose weight, ipso fatso.

As soon as I finish my pizza, I'm going to the store to get the special clothes.

Or maybe I'll just shop online.

Darwinian

||||||||||||||||||||||||||||||||||||||||||||||||||

By Lisa

I met yet another woman who's into scrapbooking, which makes me feel guilty.

I don't scrapbook.

I don't even know what scrapbooking is, or when it became a verb. I figure it means putting your pictures in a scrapbook, then labeling and dating them, or writing captions that preserve your important family memories and moments.

Doesn't that sound so nice?

If you don't do it, how could you not feel guilty?

Scrapbooking is like the pearls around June Cleaver's neck.

I want them, and I want to scrapbook. I've booked, but never scrapbooked, and I feel like it's time. Even though glue guns may be involved.

I've never shot a glue gun.

I'm in favor of glue gun control.

Any woman who scrapbooks has to be a great mother and wife, because she takes the time and care to do the little things that make life worth living.

I don't do that.

I don't take the time for the little things in life, unless they have fur. As a result, though my life is worth living, I won't remember any of it.

I took tons of photos of Daughter Francesca when she was little, but they're scattered around the house, stuck in junk drawers, cardboard boxes, and my jewelry chest. Some of the photos have made it into nice picture frames on end tables, but it's like survival of the fittest, photo-wise. The weaker ones won't make it, undoubtedly chewed up by the dogs.

This is wrong.

Nobody's family photos should die in a Darwinian struggle.

I know it seems silly to equate keeping a scrapbook with being a good mother, but still, if you don't save the photos of your children in a scrapbook, what are you saying to them?

"I love you, kid, but I don't care about your past. Let the dogs eat it."

Or:

"If it were important enough, you'd remember it."

Or:

"What's your name again?"

Technology doesn't help, either. Nowadays, I take photos with the digital camera, but they remain there, forever. I never have the time to upload them into my laptop and don't even know how to print them out. They all live inside the camera, forming their own family of family photos.

Maybe they'll find a better photo mother.

The only photos that get any currency are the ones I take with my cell phone, which I email and post. But they never get printed or saved, either, and are too blurry to be any good anyway. In fact, I've gotten way out of control with the picture-taking on my cell phone, so that all of the most important moments in my life look as if they're underwater. This will be disastrous when I'm 82, because my eyes will already suck and then I'll be looking at all those sucky photos.

Then I'll be not only a bad mother, I'll be a bad grand-mother.

This must change.

I vow to start scrapbooking.

I'm sure I can do it, I used to be kind of crafty. When I was in high school, I actually taught arts and crafts at a play-ground. It was a great summer job, playing with kids, build-ing houses out of Popsicle sticks and weaving potholders out of synthetic loops. I actually liked those potholders, but they weren't the kind of thing you'd see in Williams-Sonoma. They were too small, curled up at the edges, and generally mixed bright red with chrome yellow. I used to imagine the kids taking them home to their mothers, who threw them out immediately.

Bad mothers.

The kind who don't scrapbook.

So I went online and read some of the scrapbooking sites, to get up to speed. It turned out to be more complicated than I expected, involving The Rule of Odds and The Rule of Thirds.

I didn't know there would be rules in scrapbooking.

The Rules of Odds is that the "eye finds things arranged in odd numbers more natural and pleasing."

Who knew that your eyes followed rules? My eyes don't. They find everything natural and pleasing, especially George Clooney, and there's only one of him.

But if there were three, my eyes might like it better.

And what's the Rule of Thirds? If you draw two vertical lines and two horizontal lines on the scrapbooking page, "where those lines intersect are points of prime visual interest."

My eyes started to glaze over, and I wasn't even at the glue guns. And then I read that people who scrapbook are called scrapbookers, and I gave up.

It looked too hard.

I'll stick to being a booker.

The Moon and I

|||||||||||||||||||||||||||||||||||||||||||||||||

By Francesca

I figure, if something happens once every 372 years, it's worth staying up to see.

At least, that was my logic at 3:17 A.M., as I stood at my window and peered up at the lunar eclipse.

Last night was the first time a lunar eclipse occurred on the winter solstice since 1638. To take you back to eighth-grade Earth Science for a minute: the winter solstice is the longest night of the year, when the Earth is tilted as far away from the sun as possible. A lunar eclipse is when the moon passes directly behind the Earth, and thus the Earth blocks the sun's rays from striking the moon's surface, leaving it in shadow.

Are you bored? I don't blame you. So were all my friends when I tried to rally a few of them to stay up and watch with me. There are plenty of things my friends will gladly lose sleep over—a "surprise" Kanye concert at the Bowery, the new iPhone, the latest Harry Potter film, pretty much any party with free drinks—but natural phenomena don't generally rank among them.

But that's why I was so interested in the eclipse; anything natural in New York City is a phenomenon.

So I refused to let everyone's lack of enthusiasm dampen

mine. I felt fortunate to discover that I had a decent view of the moon from my very own bedroom window. Bolstered by Diet Coke and the lilting brogue of Craig Ferguson, I patiently awaited the evening's performance.

Around 1:30 A.M., a shadow crept over the bottom left-hand corner of the moon. I peeked out about every ten minutes to watch as the shadow took a larger and larger bite out of the white, sugar-cookie moon.

I expected the moon to go completely black when the shade passed over it, but it remained visible. Without the sun's spotlight on it, the moon's three dimensionality was easier to see. It looked like a little toy ball, hung in a schoolchild's solar system project.

Closer to 2:30 A.M., the moon became imbued with a soft red color. I looked online and came to this shaky understanding of the cause: If you were standing on the moon looking toward Earth, you would see the sunlight slipping out of sight from every point on the Earth's circumference. So essentially, the red color on the moon is a reflection of infinite sunsets.

Wow.

I wanted to tell someone, to shake someone awake and point out the window, but there was no one around. I looked over at Pip, who was stretched out on my bedspread in a Superman pose, fast asleep.

I was hoping for a howl at least.

I considered calling someone, maybe my mom, but it was too late. I held up my dinky cell phone camera for a picture, but it couldn't remotely capture it. I was sure I could find fellow amateur astronomers chattering online, but what for?

Why did I want someone to look at me looking at it? Why did I need someone to acknowledge my acknowledgment?

So I put down my laptop, my phone, and my camera, and I stood alone at my window. I decided to experience the eclipse, just for myself.

For a change.

Watching the moon's blush deepen from a pale rosewater to a dusty rouge, I was struck with the paradoxical sensation of feeling both insignificant and privileged, small and special, at the same time.

I felt small because what I was seeing put myself in perspective. Every day, I walk around and take the physical world for granted—in my world, I am the center of the universe. But at that moment, I was looking at the perfect alignment of a star, a planet, a moon, and me. I was suddenly aware of my physical position in a universe infinitely larger than myself. I was but a tiny organism, a few stories above the Earth's crust, watching the shadow of my modest planet pass over its little moon. But tiny though I might be, I was connected to that moon, and to everything beyond, all of us on the same line, tethered one to the other.

With the moon awash in sunsets, I felt the dawning of a sense of unity and peace. On that longest winter night, I felt grateful and warm.

"Lunar Eclipse" was trending on Twitter the next morning, but instead of people sharing their experience, most were re-tweeting a link to NASA's slideshow of high-tech, professional photographs. Every one of the slides showed a clearer, closer, and more vivid picture of what I saw last night.

And yet, nothing compared to the view from my window.

Big and Me

|||||||||||||||||||||||||||||||||||||||||||||||||

By Lisa

I'm in love with Big.

But in my case, Big is my Big TV.

I work all the time and keep the TV on in the background, so I'm spending every day and night with Big. This is my best marriage ever. If my third husband will be a dog, my fourth with be a Sony.

This is also the summer of every sports final in the world, including the World Cup, and bottom line, I am glued.

I mean, working.

It started with the Stanley Cup finals, and though I never watched ice hockey in my life, I started and couldn't stop. I've never seen a more exciting game in my life. Big guys skating at top speed, slamming into walls and each other, slapping pucks and faces.

Wow!

It wasn't just exciting, it was stressful. The dogs were riveted, even the cats. I defy anyone to watch only five minutes of a Stanley Cup game. Ice hockey is the potato chips of televised sports.

The Stanley Cup finals gave shape to my weeks, because games were held every other night or so, bringing an unprecedented level of excitement chez Scottoline, especially on a Wednesday night. And when the Stanley Cup finals ended, the NBA Finals began, and my chair was still warm. Of course I started watching.

I mean, working.

I had never watched an entire basketball game in my life, but I got into the basketball finals, even though I didn't care about either team. It turns out that basketball is exciting, too. Big guys running around like crazy, passing balls and throwing elbows, plus there's tattoos and celebrities. I spend a lot of time trying to figure out who has which tattoo, and also trying to catch a glimpse of Jack Nicholson. If Jack Nicholson got a tattoo, I'd be a basketball fanatic.

All of which flowed naturally into soccer's World Cup finals, another sport I never cared about until my deadline. Now I have soccer on all the time, and boy, is that fun to watch!

I mean, work.

Big guys running around at speed, kicking a ball, their sweaty hair flying, and all of them superhot, with exotic names. I bet they even have accents, though who cares if they talk? The hotness and the accents are what's keeping me glued to soccer, and the only drawback is the air horns. Sorry, I can't work with the constant air horns. It sounds like emergency sports. I say, let the spectators have the horns and turn the sound down, for the authors on deadline.

Of course, my nonstop viewing of sports I don't care about has led to a considerable weight gain. This isn't that surprising. It happens when you're happily married, and Big solved this problem for me, too.

I was scrolling around the onscreen TV Guide the other day

and came across Fitness TV, then clicked through to Yoga. I found Beginning Yoga and decided to give it a whirl, then and there. After all, I was already dressed in loose-fitting clothes, as that's all I ever wear and had never before thought of as exercise gear.

Anyway, I set my laptop and pretzels aside, got out of my chair, and put a bath towel on the rug and tried to imitate the lady on the TV, herself a pretzel stick. Our session started with sitting and breathing, which is my kind of exercise, and I was really good at it, not to brag.

I bet you can do it, too.

Try it at home.

Sit down. Breathe in. Breathe out.

Yay!

Then we moved onto Sun Salutes, which is basically standing, breathing, and waving your hands in a way that looks like a little kid doing ballet but is in fact a greeting of a major planet.

Hi, Sun!

Hot enough for ya?

This would be yogic humor.

This pose got the cats' attention, and then we segued into Downward Dog, which got the dogs', for obvious reasons. I was upside down, red-faced, and already sweating, with my butt in the air, and all the dogs came over, sniffing, nuzzling, and licking crumbs off my shirt and shorts.

You know you're in trouble when your clothes are delicious.

Luckily, Big isn't complaining.

What a guy.

Birthday Wish

||||||||||||||||||||||||||||||||||||||||||||||

By Lisa

There's nothing like your birthday to take you back to your beginnings, so it made sense that I spent mine in Ascoli-Piceno, Italy. The town is two thousand years old, and being there made me feel like an infant, as I was turning a mere fifty-five.

For my next birthday, I'm going to Stonehenge.

Then the more I travel, the younger I'll get.

Ascoli-Piceno was the hometown of my grandparents on my father's side, Mary and Antonio Scottoline, before they emigrated to America. My father and brother had been there once, but I never had, which is something I'll explain later.

Ascoli-Piceno lies on the Tronto River in the Le Marche region, in the middle of Italy. The trip from Rome took four hours by car, and the highway passed by insanely picturesque farmhouses and olive groves until it narrowed to a skinny road with hairpin turns that wound around mountains. I kept my eyes closed for the mountain part. Everyone thought I was sleeping, but I was terrified.

I like my hairpins in my hair, only.

I was traveling with Daughter Francesca in a bite-size Fiat packed with my Italian editor, publicist, and translator, which makes me sound like I roll with an entourage to rival a rapper.

I don't, except when they're kind enough to promote my book in Italy, and because my publisher is also from Ascoli-Piceno, it was his great idea to take me there.

You may be wondering why it took a complete stranger to bring me home.

So am I.

The oldest section of the town is hewn from travertine marble taken from the surrounding mountains, and it lends a lovely gray cast to the medieval-scale houses that line the cobblestone streets, many only as wide as an alley. A town square called the Piazza del Popolo is the heart of the city, and it's ringed by a breezy arched walkway, the gorgeous Cathedral of Sant'Emidio, and a historic Town Hall. Wikipedia says the piazza is "considered one of the most beautiful in Italy," and for once, Wikipedia is accurate.

The day I was there, the piazza was filled with a team of seventy-five men and women who were rehearsing their flag-throwing for a *La Quintana,* a jousting competition to be held the next month. The flags were the team colors, bright yellow and clear blue, the hues of the Italian sun and sky. We watched the silk flags swirl, dip, and fly though the air, each movement timed perfectly to the beat of music played on ancient trumpets.

It was an amazing way to spend a birthday, but I was missing something.

It was over ten years ago that my father and brother planned their trip to Ascoli-Piceno, and they asked Francesca and me to go with them, but I said no. I'd wished I could go but I thought I had too much work, and a deadline. They came home full of pictures and stories, and they'd met a slew of relatives who'd fed them for three days. My father got choked up when he told me that he saw his mother's face in the features of his cousins, and how moved he was by walking the same cobblestones his parents had left behind, for the streets of gold in America. He laughed when he remembered that his mother had always wanted to move back to Ascoli-Piceno, even after living in Philadelphia for thirty years, because the food was better.

I told my father I'd go to Ascoli-Piceno with him someday, and I meant it. He said he'd wait, but cancer got to him first.

And so I found myself lighting a candle for him in the Cathedral of Sant'Emidio. It was a bitter moment, full of regret. I hadn't gone with him, but I wished I had. I wished I still could. It was an unhappy sort of birthday wish, and a weird sort of birthday candle.

Lisa and her father, Frank Scottoline

I'd thought work was more important. It wasn't.

I'd thought I had forever. I didn't.

Life has a deadline, too.

Then I realized that maybe I had gotten my birthday wish, after all. Because standing at the cool altar of the stone church, in the place where my father had stood, and where his father before him had stood, and even his father before *him* had stood, I felt connected, still. To him, and to them all. And I stood there with my own daughter and could see in her glistening eyes that she would come back here someday, maybe with her own children, to this very same spot, which had existed for thousands of years and would continue to exist for a thousand more.

Happy Birthday, to me.

And *grazie,* Dad.

Love you.

Life in the Not-So-Fast Lane

||||||||||||||||||||||||||||||||||||||||||||||||||

By Lisa

I was driving home last night on the highway when that old Eagles song came on the radio, "Life in the Fast Lane." At the time, I was in the middle lane.

Ironic.

I love the middle lane. If I could live my life in the middle lane, I would.

I avoid the fast lane at all costs, because I'm not that kind of girl.

I belong in the middle lane because I follow the rules and drive the speed limit. I don't like to go too fast and I don't like to go too slow. I'm Goldilocks, on wheels.

Also the middle lane is the safest. I like to keep my options open, so if there's an accident, I can escape left or right. This reminds me of my divorces from Thing One and Thing Two. The middle lane is for people who understand the necessity for Plan B on the turnpike of life.

Life in the fast lane is too risky for me. Cars could cross over the divider. Also highway debris, or low-flying geese.

The slow lane is equally treacherous. Trees could topple onto me. Deer could dart in front of me. And don't get me started on falling rocks. You ever drive by those FALLING ROCKS signs?

They're always placed next to a mountain composed entirely of loose boulders, which are held in place by chicken wire.

This is straight-up crazy.

Take it from me, chicken wire doesn't have a chance against falling rocks. I know because chicken wire doesn't even hold back chickens. I had to replace my chicken wire because one of my hens, Princess Ida, chewed it up, determined to fly the coop. In fact, if you ask me, we should put Princess Ida in charge of falling rocks.

She could stop them with one wing tied behind her back.

The only time the middle lane becomes dangerous is at night, when truckers get cranky. Let me first say that I love truckers. They're the only men left who still flirt with me, and I suspect that's because I look my best from a distance.

If you're driving on I-95 and I'm driving on I-78, I'm super-hot.

Also I love truckers because they send me lots of email, telling me that they like listening to my books on tape while they drive. It turns out that truckers are some of the best-read people around, which shows that you can't judge an audiobook by its cover.

And if they read me, even better. I love anybody who reads me. Except when they try to run me off the road.

Truckers have to use the middle lane, and they tend to line up behind me, flashing their massive headlights to pressure me out of their way. This happened again last night, when it was proverbially dark and stormy. I was driving the speed limit, but the trucker kept honking and flashing his lights. I would have switched lanes, but the fast lane was full of speeders avoiding geese.

And the slow lane was clogged with people distracted by Falling Rocks.

Nobody would let me in, which was obvious to everyone but the trucker, who kept honking and tailgating me until my car flooded with light from his high beams. His big rig even had those scary shark-teeth, and a teddy bear was roped to his grill like a hostage.

Maybe Stephen King was driving.

My fingers tightened on the wheel, and I kept looking left and right, but couldn't switch lanes.

Still, HONK! HONK!

At first, I felt bullied. Then angry. And finally, I admit it, I got so scared that I couldn't even flip him the bird.

In time, I saw my opening and got out of his way, then he sped past me, spraying water and road dirt.

Maybe he didn't like my audiobook?

No matter.

In time, I got back where I belonged, cruising calmly.

Whatever, Eagles.

Life in The Middle Lane has its own rewards.

It's Not The Heat

|||||||||||||||||||||||||||||||||||||||||||||||||||

By Lisa

Hot enough for ya?

That's right. I like to talk about the weather. More accurately, I'm fascinated by the weather. We begin where I begin every day, on weather.com.

For me, weather.com is online porn.

I don't know if it's because I'm in the middle of writing a book, and I'm not sure where the plot is going or what the characters will do, but I love that if I log onto weather.com, I get answers.

Answers, answers, and more answers.

I click to weather.com, then click again to Hourly, to break down the weather for the coming day, complete with adorable pictures of shiny suns or thumbnail thunderbolts. At a glance, first thing in the morning, I can find out that it will be ninety-two degrees at 11:15 A.M. today.

Wow!

Where else can you get someone to foretell your future, humidity index included?

Come to think of it, that's what I love most about weather .com. It can tell all sorts of information about the future with precision, and I want to know everything I can about the future, especially if it includes when my hair will frizz.

For example, once I find out that the sunshine today will morph to light rain at 3:17 P.M., I click over to the Mosquito Index. Yes, on weather.com, you can click to find out when you're most likely to get bitten by a mosquito, which turns out to be between 5:06 P.M. and 6:37 A.M., tomorrow morning. And tonight, if you want to know, the Mosquito Activity will be between None and Limited, as opposed to the top of the scale, which is Very High. You don't want to plan your picnic for when the mosquitoes are at their worst, which is Really Frigging Annoying.

And on the Mosquito Index page, there's even a sidebar asking, Want To Know When The Fish Are Biting?

And suddenly, I do!

I want to know when the fish are biting, even though I don't fish. In fact, I didn't even know they bite.

I click my way to the Fishing Forecast, where you can search by zip code or by lake, and this astounds me. Weather.com can tell you when the fish will be biting in a particular lake?

How great is that?

It bodes well for our country, if we can foretell when fish will be biting in Lake Whatever, and at what time. If we can do that, we can put a man on the moon.

Or back on the moon.

Or at least make my hair not frizz.

The first lake that pops into my mind is Lake Winnipesaukee, because it's mentioned in a movie I love, *What About Bob?* Of course, Lake Winnipesaukee is impossible to spell, which is a joke in the movie, so to get the right spelling, I have to navigate to Google, where I plug in the wrong spelling and it asks me, DID YOU MEAN . . . and supplies the right spelling.

Yes, Google, I did mean that. What you said. Thanks for saving my face, online. Google is almost as smart as weather.com. It can't tell the future, but it can read your mind.

Anyway, I go back to the Fishing Forecast, plug Lake Winnipesaukee into the lake search, and am rewarded with a multicolored wiggly line showing that today, the Lake Winnipesaukee fish will be biting the most between 12:01 P.M. and 2:06 P.M.

Ouch.

If I were you, I'd stay away.

And the same webpage also informs me that the Moon Phase tonight will be Waxing Gibbous.

See? Toldja! Answers, answers, and more answers.

I'm so happy to know this about the moon, though I have no idea what Waxing Gibbous means. I could find out, but I don't need to to marvel at how great it is to know it, precisely.

And I'm not talking about horoscope-level precision. I'm talking, real, no-joke, scientific-type precision. In my experience, weather.com is never wrong. Or if it's wrong, it changes its forecast right away, which is still kosher.

Politicians do it all the time.

Moms Say the Darndest

||||||||||||||||||||||||||||||||||||||||||||||||||

By Lisa

Everyone takes different risks in life. Some people defuse bombs. Other people juggle knives. I give a microphone to Mother Mary, in front of 350 of my readers.

If you ask me, it's safer to skydive than to ask Mother Mary to speak in front of an audience. You never know what she's going to say. Remember kids say the darndest things?

Mother Mary says the darndest things, too.

Here's what I've observed. When you're young, up to the age of seven, you can say anything you want and people will think it's adorable. Everybody loves the honesty of children. They get automatic immunity.

Same way when you're older, over the age of seventy. You can say anything you damn well please and everybody will think it's great. You've earned the right to be completely honest and get out of jail free.

It's between the ages of seven and seventy that you get sued, slapped, or fired from your network TV job, but that's not the point herein.

The point is that Mother Mary never met a microphone she didn't like.

And I made the first mistake, by inviting her to my Big

Book Club party. Francesca came, too, and we held it at the house, with a tent, catered food, music, and a full floor show.

Well, the floor show is me talking about myself. Just like here. And at my signings. I begin by giving a speech about myself, then I segue into a question-and-answer period about me.

Now you know why I'm divorced twice.

I invite book clubs who have read my most recent novel, and I've been doing this for the past five years. I started with 23 book clubs, and the party has grown to 112 book clubs over two days, and boy, am I happy. I'm thrilled that book clubs like my novels, and I appreciate their reading me, which is the purpose of the party, to say a very personal thank-you.

In fact, thank you, readers everywhere.

I don't think of the book club members as my customers, but in a sense, they are. So you have to imagine the panic that squeezes my heart like a fist when Mother Mary goes off script, keeps the microphone, and tells the crowd the following:

That I hurried her off the toilet when it was time to come to the party.

That I hurry her around in general.

That I can be bossier than you think.

That I was on the scale, cursing, that very morning.

That I bought her her hearing aids and make her wear them because I want to get my money's worth.

That I scratch my back with the backscratcher the wrong way. I do it from the bottom and reach up, but you're supposed to do it from top and reach down. Then Mother Mary actually demonstrates the correct procedure, with a backscratcher she wields like a scepter. She wears black stretch pants, her lab coat, and a thirty-year-old bra.

Mother Mary never met a microphone she didn't like.

Please, visualize amongst yourselves.

By the way, I forgot to tell you that Mother Mary took to wearing a lab coat around about age seventy-five. I'm not sure why or how, as she has no medical training, but she bought one at the dollar store and decided it was a good look for her. So now she's Dr. Mom.

Literally.

But back to the story. She tells the crowd that I didn't talk at all for the first few years of my life and they took me to several doctors, who thought I was learning disabled. But when I finally spoke, at age three, I said, "I want a cookie."

At this point, I wrest the microphone from her arthritic little hand. I offer no explanation for my belated speech, except that I really wanted a cookie.

And I still do.

What does it mean if your first word is *carbohydrates*?

(Maybe that you'll be cursing on the scale.)

Well, it gets worse.

There's nothing about me she doesn't know, and there's nothing about me she won't say, so after I've delighted the crowd with my speech, quips, and anecdotes to illustrate how great I am, my mother takes the floor and disillusions them by telling them everything about the real me. This defeats the purpose of the entire tax-deductible party, and by the time the book club members leave, several are looking at me funny and one advises that I should let my mother take all the time she needs on the toilet.

"How'd I do?" Mother Mary asks, after everyone has gone.

"Terrific!" Francesca tells her.

And oddly, I agree.

Not Under My Roof

By Francesca

I was raised right, and I have my mother to thank. I used to gripe about some of her rules and chores, but in the end, she was usually right, and I carried those lessons with me. Now I have a relatively clean, tidy, well-run household.

Until my mom comes to visit.

Something strange happens when my mother stays with me—we swap roles. It's like my apartment is a wormhole to bizarro world, where I am my mother, and my mother is teenage me.

Because my mom is within driving distance, she has no imperative to pack neatly, so she always comes in like a bag lady and basically explodes with stuff.

In her defense, my apartment is small enough that any added things constitute a natural disaster.

Yet somehow, she also never has a suitable outfit for whatever our main activity is and must borrow one from me.

But I can't complain. I've raided her closet since I was fifteen, so I owe her on this one.

I think my mom's favorite thing about staying with me, beyond the money saved or the quality time with boring ol' me, is that she can bring Little Tony and Peach. I love to see them, and so does my dog, Pip, but three toy-sized dogs in a toy-sized apartment create a surprising amount of dirt.

Think Dust Bowl with dog hair.

There was a time when my mom and I had five dogs and a cat, so we are old pros at pet-hair management. At home, we have L.L. Bean furniture liners that must cover the sofa and armchair anytime we are not sitting on them, or company isn't over. When I was still living at home, if I so much as got up to go to the bathroom, my mom would nag me about forgetting to cover the couch.

In my apartment, I have a ratty blanket for the same purpose. I thought my mom would be proud. But instead, she ignored it.

"Mom," I said, replacing the blanket for the second time that day. "You have to make sure the blanket is covering the couch cushions, especially after the dogs come in from a walk."

"They're not that dirty."

"Yes, they are."

My mom rolled her eyes at me and complied.

Now was that so hard?

Another night, we were about to head out to see a movie. I was waiting by the door while my mom gathered her things.

"Okay, ready," she said.

"You left the kitchen light on."

"I know. I left it on for the dogs."

What, do they have a lot of reading to do?

"It's wasteful," I said.

With an exaggerated sigh, my mom trudged back to the kitchen and turned off the light.

"What's with the attitude?" I asked. But I could hear her voice saying it, even as the words left my mouth.

Scary.

When I was younger, another of my daily chores was setting the table. There was a right way to do it, and that was to clear the table, wipe the table down with a damp sponge, and set it with a full set of silverware—fork, knife, and spoon, no matter what my mom was serving for dinner.

On my mom's last visit, I convinced her to take a night off of restaurants or takeout and let me make dinner. I wanted to show her that I can take care of myself, because like any good Italian mother, she never thinks I'm eating well or enough. Since I cooked, she set the table.

I brought over the salad bowl and saw big paper towels by each plate.

"I have napkins," I said.

"Eh, I didn't know where they were. This was easier," she replied.

Paper towels were always a forbidden shortcut in our house, but I bit my tongue. My bewilderment increased when I lifted the towel and saw only a fork and a knife beneath it.

"I'm gonna have a Diet Coke," my mom said. "Do you want one?"

"Sure, and while you're up, can you grab us two spoons?"

"We don't need them."

"It's good to have them, just in case."

"In case of what?"

"In case my mom comes over!"

And we both laughed.

Uncle Sam

|||||||||||||||||||||||||||||||||||||||||||||||||

By Lisa

Thank God for our government, which just sued a yogurt company.

Whew.

Don't worry, America, they're on it.

You may think that we have bigger problems for government to fix, but you'd be wrong.

Silly wabbit. Government can't fix anything.

A yogurt company may sound harmless, as compared with thieving banks and Charlie Sheen, but appearances can be deceiving.

Luckily, we don't have to watch out for ourselves, thanks to Uncle Sam. He's a good uncle, even though he never gives us a dollar at Christmas, like my Uncle Ed used to. I loved Uncle Ed, but Uncle Sam is from the Other Side of the Family.

Every family has an Other Side.

It's either Your Mother's Side or Your Father's Side, but we all know what we mean when we say the Other Side.

Them.

Not us.

Uncle Sam sued the yogurt company for claiming that Activia yogurt would make people more regular, if they ate it once a day. The government said that the company was exaggerating with its ads, because people would probably have to eat Activia three times a day to be more regular.

Thanks, government. Because who would ever guess that ads exaggerate anything?

Hmm.

For example, I believed an ad for a lipstick that said it would get me a man.

But it didn't.

And I believed an ad for sneakers that would make me thinner, but they didn't. And my face soap didn't make me younger, and my car didn't change my life. Obviously, I was cheated, and Uncle Sam needs to step in. I want ads for things we can trust.

Like politicians.

As for Activia, let's get real.

Have you ever tasted Activia? I have, and I love it. It's delicious. A creamy vanilla flavor, light and perfect. It's so good, it's criminal. In fact, maybe that yogurt company got off easy, only being sued.

They should go to jail.

I never endorse products, and this still isn't a product endorsement, because honestly, you shouldn't buy Activia. You know why? Because if you do, you'll never stop eating it. You'll be so regular, you won't ever leave the house.

If you follow.

Come to think of it, now that our government has established that you need three Activia a day to be regular, it should move quickly to find out what happens if you eat fifty-seven a day.

Because I could.

But it's not my fault. It's the yogurt company's fault. Because it puts Activia in little containers, which makes me eat more than one.

Hell, they practically stick that spoon in my hand.

And if that weren't bad enough, the company sells Activia in packs of six, all stuck together. It simply resists being pulled apart. In one sitting, I could eat six, no problem. Activia is a six-pack for girls.

If this keeps up, I'll have an Activia belly.

Finally, I appreciate that Uncle Sam is so concerned about my health and welfare, especially my bowel movements.

Thanks, Unc!

Some people dislike governmental intrusion, but not me. Privacy is overrated. I don't value it at all, as you know if you read this column.

I'm happy my government's up my butt.

And the best part is that the yogurt company had to settle the lawsuit, paying the government some $21 million, which I'm sure will be put to excellent use. Uncle Sam may not give us money at Christmas, but with luck we'll get a really nice screwdriver.

So we're screwed.

I think that $21 million will go far toward paying off the federal deficit, which is now at $13 trillion. After all, you have to start somewhere.

There are a lot of drops in a bucket.

Mathlete

||||||||||||||||||||||||||||||||||||||||||||||||||||

By Lisa

I was never good at math, but I figured it didn't matter. Unfortunately, it does, at least when you make cranberry sauce.

And it's more than just math, it's science, too. I figured I'd never need to know anything about volume, but I do. Again, I was wrong, when it comes to cranberry sauce.

Cranberry sauce is high-maintenance, for a condiment.

We begin with what happens to me every holiday meal, when cranberry sauce demands to be made. For some reason, I never end up with the 12-ounce bag of Ocean Spray cranberries that dummyproofs the entire process. It has the recipe right on it, and all you have to do is follow it, dump the cranberries and sugar into the boiling water, and you're good to go.

Plus I get extra credit for making my own cranberry sauce from scratch, and not just opening the can and making it look homemade by chopping it up with a fork.

That's beneath me.

Sort of.

Obviously, I'm not a high-rent kind of cook. I own fancy cookbooks, but the recipe on the Ocean Spray bag is as reliably awesome as the one for chocolate chip cookies on the

Hershey's bag. If these companies ever change their wrapping, I can't cook.

But anyway, the store is always out of the Ocean Spray bag by the time I get there, so I have to buy whatever overpriced organic cranberries are on hand, and unfortunately, they're always too pretentious to have a recipe on the package.

And this time, I ended up with a plastic container of artisanal cranberries whose label said that it contained one dry quart of cranberries.

Huh?

I don't know what a quart of cranberries is. A quart of milk, I'm familiar. But cranberries?

I have a vague understanding that there's some kind of difference between dry measures and liquid measures, but I never understood what the difference was. For this reason, I own a bewildering array of Pyrex measuring cups, but I have no idea if they measure dry stuff or wet stuff, or if that matters.

That would be the science part.

So I thumb through my fancy cookbooks on Thanksgiving Day to find a cranberry-sauce recipe, but they're too full of themselves to help me out with such a basic recipe, and even *The Joy of Cooking* doesn't have one.

Now I know I'm in trouble.

If it's not in *The Joy of Cooking,* my cooking is joyless.

I'm fresh out of joy.

So I go online to try and find a cranberry sauce recipe, and every single recipe tells you to use 12 ounces of cranberries. Because everybody but me has that Ocean Spray bag.

Ocean Spray intends world domination.

In fact, Ocean Spray is the Microsoft of cranberry companies.

Of course, the Ocean Spray recipe is on its website, and it specifies 12 ounces of cranberries. But I have no idea how many ounces are in one dry quart, or the other way around. I know it sounds dumb, but I don't even know which is bigger. Or heavier. Or wetter. Or dryer.

You see the problem.

So I type the following question into Google: "How many ounces are in one dry quart?" And a bunch of links pops up, so I click on the first, from wiki answers, and it reads:

32.

Blink. Blink blink.

I don't even know what that means, as far as the recipe goes. Hoping to get a clue, I click on the next link, which purports to answer the same exact question. And its answer, also from wiki answers, is:

5.

Uh oh.

Now I officially don't understand. There are either 5 or 32 ounces in one dry quart.

And the only person dumber than me is this wiki dude.

So now I'm starting to panic, and I go from one link to the next, eventually falling into a wormhole of conversion tables, where I encounter words like drams and deciliters, and I learn that one firkin is equal to 34.069 liters.

I had no idea. I should have listened in firkin class.

And do you know how many liters are in a hogshead?

If you said 238.48, you win a can of cranberry sauce.

Which is what I'm buying, as soon as I get my coat on.

Oprah and Einstein

||||||||||||||||||||||||||||||||||||||||||||||||||

By Lisa

Oprah is the genius who coined the term "aha moment," wherein you realize something about yourself, usually something that makes you feel smarter.

Me, I remember an aha moment that made me feel dumber.

It happened a while ago, at the time of the awful oil spill in the Gulf of Mexico, and I was on an airplane in front of two men who spent the entire three hours trying to figure out a way to stop the spill.

And then, that's when I thought, aha!

I'm not smart enough to fix an oil spill.

But before we go further, let me be clear:

I was sad about the oil spill, and I knew it wasn't a laughing matter. I used to read everything I could on the subject, because I cared.

All I'm saying is that I had no idea how to stop it. I don't know how to plug a hole in the Earth. I can barely work my BlackBerry.

I admired these men, who had so many ideas. That's the kind of can-do attitude that makes America great.

Only problem is, I figured out then, I can't do.

Rather, I can do lots of things, but I know, as sure as shootin', I can't do *that*.

Consider the men behind me, on the plane. They weren't engineers or anything, and they weren't friends before the flight. I know this because I heard the whole conversation, from take-off to landing. I always eavesdrop, especially when I fly. In fact, nobody's secrets are safe from me, anywhere. I'm nosy. I listen when it looks like I'm reading. If you see me in a restaurant and you think I didn't hear your conversation, you're wrong.

And if you ask me if I overheard and I say no, I'm lying.

The men on the plane struck up a conversation that started with how-about-that-oil-spill and turned into a brainstorming session about plugs, cantilevers, sleeves, gloves, and valves.

My head was spinning.

These were normal guys. I won't tell you what they do for a living, even though I know, in case they read this. Also, it's against my rules. Even though I listen to your secrets, I don't repeat them.

I keep secrets secret.

Anyway, not only did these guys try to solve the oil spill, they were fascinated by their own conversation. I know this because at the end of the flight, they exchanged business cards, which is something men do when they like each other.

Bottom line, I was happy for them, but I'm not like them.

If I think about the things I can talk about for three hours and be fascinated, there are many. Kids, family, friends, dogs, cats, food, ponies, carbohydrates, and food.

Did I say food?

Food.

But not levers. Ever.

I mean, some awful company punched a hole in the Earth and now it's leaking. How do you repair a planet?

I don't know.

Why not?

I'm no Einstein.

Or Oprah.

Most of the time, the only thing floating around in my head are jingles from TV commercials. I never forget a jingle. I even remember, "See the USA in your Chevrolet." And, "My baloney has a first name." Plus I would still like to buy the world a Coke and keep it company.

There are current jingles stuck in my head, too. The Kindle song about "I love you" and "You stole my heart" and "1,2,3," runs on a loop in my brain, probably in the jingle lobe. In another mood, I can sing the Subway "Five, five dollar, five dollar foot long" song. I sing it all the time, wiping my kitchen counter, washing my hair, unloading the dishwasher.

I even know what number to call for Empire Flooring.

I bet you do, too.

So here's what I'm thinking:

You know who's smart enough to plug the hole in the ocean? The people who write jingles.

That would be my only idea to fix the oil spill.

Call Empire Flooring.

I bet they cover it with a nice carpet.

Aha!

Toys in the Attic

IIIIIIIIIIIIIIIIIIIIIIIIIIIIIIIIIIIIIIIIIIIIIIIIIII

By Lisa

I just read about the people who found a vase in their attic, which was sold to Chinese buyers for $86 million.

How does this happen, and why is my attic so inferior?

I don't understand stories like that. They make me totally crazy. It happens all the time. People find stuff in their attic that turns out to be worth a fortune. Like a map that has a Rembrandt underneath. Or a calendar that covers the last copy of the Declaration of Independence.

Who are these people? Where do they live? And how do they get the best attics ever?

Here's what's in my attic: Old books, but not so old as to be worth money. Old clothes, but not so old to be worth money. Old chairs, but not so old to be worth money. In fact, I'm older than anything in my attic, and even I'm not worth that much money.

Evidently, only inanimate objects acquire value as they get older. People just get called seniors.

Curse you, other people's attics! Also the social security system, ageism, and society in general!

See how I get, from these attic stories?

Crazy!

I have an idea. Maybe if we take the seniors and put them in the attic, they'll be worth something when they come out.

Let's find out.

Try this at home. Go, quick! Hustle Mom and Dad upstairs, right now. Push their sorry asses into the attic. Slam the door, lock it, and set the timer for 300 years. Then take them out and sell them.

Too dark?

Let's go back to the aforementioned vase. I looked at a photo of it online. It's cute, as vases go, and if I'd found it in my lame and inferior attic, I wouldn't have thought it was anything special. It's blue, yellow, and green, and has two fish on the side.

That's 42 mil a fish.

My guess is they're goldfish.

Of real gold.

The vase in the attic was from the eighteenth century, and to be precise, the Qianlong Dynasty.

Who knew? If I'd looked at that vase, I would have said Ming. Definitely, Ming. As in Ming a Ding Ding, which was the favorite dynasty of Frank Sinatra.

But it was Qianlong, which I'd never heard of. I only know Qianshort.

Still, I shouldn't feel bad about not identifying the vase correctly. After all, the people who found the vase in their amazing attic took it to an auction house, where they were told by the experts that it was worth $2 million.

Chump change.

But later, in an auction that lasted half an hour, the bidding went up to $70 million. That's over 2 million bucks a minute.

Time really is money.

By the way, if you're wondering how the number got from $70 million to the final $86 million, the difference was the commission that went to the auction house and the tax on the commission.

That's a good commission, no? I can't divide that fast, but it sounds like 393,838 percent. Which I suppose is reasonable, for underestimating the value of the vase by $84 million.

You get what you pay for.

Reportedly, the auctioneer was surprised at the final selling price.

Ya think?

He said that there had been indications that the buyers, who were from China, had lots of money to spend, but "nothing like this."

Really?

This auctioneer has to be the most clueless person on the planet. Last time I checked online, our federal government had borrowed about $2 trillion from the Chinese.

And I'm sure we can pay them back, no problem.

If we just find the right attics.

Hardwired

|||||||||||||||||||||||||||||||||||||||||||||||||

By Lisa

There was an article in the newspaper the other day that scared me. No, it wasn't about carbohydrates.

It was about our brains, and the gist was that by going online and cruising lots of different websites, we're actually changing the wiring in our brains, and this will result in an inability to concentrate and . . .

Huh?

Where was I?

What?

Uh oh.

This is bad news. Five minutes ago, I was supposed to be working, but I took a break to go online. I stopped at all my favorite gossip websites, like perezhilton.com, people.com, and the superficial.com, then I moved on to gawker.com and gofugyourself.com.

I'm not making that last one up. It's about fashion, as you would guess if you knew how fussy I am about which sweatpants to wear.

I also visit work-related websites, like galleycat.com and publishersweekly.com, and I post on Facebook and Twitter, too.

Friend me. Follow me. This way we can get to know each another without changing out of our sweatpants.

I make lots of other local stops on my train ride through the Internet, and my track winds around and around in circles, does a few loop-de-loops, zooms around a cloverleaf and spells out CALL ME, GEORGE CLOONEY before it returns to the station.

And this will mirror the wiring in my brain?

I'm tempted to say it's mind-blowing, but that's the point.

Plus it's unfair, because the punishment doesn't fit the crime. Everybody deserves a break from work now and then, according to federal law and McDonald's.

You deserve a break today. At least six times today.

So how can it be fair that what you do during your break can break your brain?

That's like making a funny face and having your face freeze that way. And if you ever wished that on anybody, I hope you're happy now. Our brains are all messed up because of you.

The article even had a Test Your Focus interactive, so I took the test, which involved red and blue bars in various formations. I went with my best guess between Yes and No, and scored a -.33 percent, which seemed pretty good to me, considering that I didn't understand the directions.

I couldn't concentrate.

To make things worse, imagine you're a middle-aged woman.

Stop screaming.

It's not funny.

It takes a real man to be a middle-aged woman.

If you follow.

Anyway, all middle-aged women know that something happens to the brain after fifty years of age. I even read an article about it, but I can't remember where. Or someone told me, what's-her-name. And I think the article said something about declining hormone levels causing a decrease in brain function. It talked about menopause creating confusion, a wandering mind, and "brain fog."

Or something like that.

It was hard to pay attention. At the time, I was daydreaming.

About you-know-who.

Also I like my fog in the air, not between my ears. Weather, stay out of my head.

To return to topic, all I know is, menopause is bad news, brain-wise.

Consider the implications.

What this means is that those of us at a certain age have a double whammy, when it comes to the computer. In other words, if you're cruising the Internet without estrogen, you should stop right now.

Step away from the laptop.

You won't understand anything you read. And even if you did, you won't remember it.

You're a goner, cognitively speaking.

You'll fare no better, offline. One of the articles said that brain fog can roll in at any time, and "women find themselves often worrying whether or not they have forgotten to turn the iron off."

Heh heh.

Silly women, who forget to put the butter churn away, or

leave their darning needles all over the floor, where the un-
wary can step on them, getting a hole that needs . . . darning?

Darn it!

Well, I, for one, never worry about turning the iron off,
because I never turn the iron on. In fact, I don't own an iron.
And between the iron and the laptop, I'll choose the latter. In
a pinch, you can press your sweatpants with a laptop.

Don't ask me how I know.

Bank Angst

|||||||||||||||||||||||||||||||||||||||||||||||||||

By Francesca

As a young writer starting out, my number one fear in life is not having money. Money for rent, money for food, money for my dog's food, and occasionally money for those boots that make my legs look four inches longer than they are.

I can stand to skip a few meals anyway.

But you know what my number two fear is?

Managing my money.

And I don't even mean fancy stuff like investing in mutual funds or something. I don't have money for that sort of thing.

Not after those boots.

I get nervous and intimidated by the easy stuff. Just walking to the bank gives me the willies. Even tasks that should ease my mind are anxiety-inducing, like depositing a check. When I got my first major check after moving to New York, I took it to my local bank, met with an employee to open an account, and offered the check as my first deposit into my savings.

"Oh, let me show you our new check deposit function at the ATM," he said.

"We can't just do it now?" I asked.

"I could, but the ATM is much faster and easier. And no envelopes!"

What's wrong with envelopes? I like the security of an envelope's embrace. I even like that it's sealed with a spitty kiss.

I would seal it in my blood if it made my money any safer.

But I was too submissive to object, so I allowed myself to be marched over to the ATM machine. Following his instructions, I obediently swiped my card and punched in my pin. The machine prompted me to insert my check.

I looked at the banker for reassurance, still clutching my check.

"Just put it in!"

As soon as the check's perforated edge touched the ATM's steely lip, it was sucked inside the hungry mouth of the machine.

I was surprised it didn't burp.

"Confirm the amount," he said, pointing. "Is that right?"

I don't know, is it? Was that the right cent amount at the end? If I couldn't remember the precise cent amount, why did I think my memory was correct about the dollar amount? I was thrown into a tailspin of doubt, and the only paper to confirm it was now within the beast's metallic innards.

"Cool how it eats it up, huh?"

Cool?

I felt queasy.

The other source of *agida*? Online banking. But I survived the journey of setting up my manifold security settings, so I figure I might as well use it.

Still, I'm terrified of messing up. Whenever it's time to pay my bills online or transfer funds, I become neurotic. I clear my table of everything but my laptop, I turn up the lights, I turn off any music or TV. Environment conditions must be optimal for my uninterrupted focus as I slowly read each page and deliberately click on each command.

Everything about it is too instantaneous for my comfort level. For example, why is my online banking site the only website on earth that does not have a confirmation page before paying money? I can't buy lip-gloss from Sephora.com without it confirming the contents of my cart, my Beauty Insider Rewards points, and my shipping preference. With online banking, I can mistakenly pay my cable bill an amount with an extra zero in a single click.

That's never actually happened, but it could!

Certain online features are just needlessly threatening. Right at the top of my account page, it says, "INSUFFICIENT FUNDS" in big capital letters, and I always think, also in big capital letters, "OMG MY BANK ACCOUNT HAS BEEN EMPTIED!" before I read below where it says, "To help prevent overdrafting your account, we automatically send you an email when your account has insufficient funds."

You really want to help me, online banking? Don't alert me to my alerts in such an alarming font size. It overdrafts my blood pressure.

Whatever competency I have achieved with online banking has only crippled me with paper banking. In the rare instance when I have to write out an actual check, I must double check every step to make sure I did it right, which makes me feel like a complete idiot.

Some people can forge checks; I aim to get my own signature in the right place.

But kidding aside, is the Memo part important?

I save every piece of literature from my bank, and I organize all mailings in an OCD folder system. I get anxious right before I open my account statements, even when I know I haven't overspent. I feel like some terrible revelation lies behind the envelope.

Maybe I don't like envelopes after all.

I'm terrified of identity theft, so I've thought of the most convoluted passwords—letters, numbers, words, acronyms, palindromes. No one is guessing my password.

Least of all me.

The flaw in my strategy was clear when I was studying abroad in Italy. I needed to get cash from an ATM there, only to find that their number keypads do not have letters like American ones do. I remember my PIN number in part by remembering a word. I had no idea what the numbers alone were.

Aha! I pulled out my cell phone to use its number pad as a guide, only to be reminded that the BlackBerry has a QWERTY keyboard, not the old phone one.

Stupida.

So there I was, sitting in a Roman café, trying to re-create the old phone keypad on a napkin.

The number 1 has no letters on it, does it? 2 has ABC . . .

Finally, it occurred to me to Google image search "American ATM keypad" on my BlackBerry's mobile web. I felt like some sort of foreign criminal, but it worked.

And they say technology makes our lives more efficient.

But I guess my anxiety about money is a normal part of starting out on my own. Everything gets easier with practice.

Now if I could just make a bit more to practice with.

Tempus Fugit

|||||||||||||||||||||||||||||||||||||||||||||||||

By Lisa

Time flies.

Some of you will say it's a cliché, and others will say it's a proverb, but it doesn't matter which to me. I'm not too cool for school, and have no complaint with clichés. A great thing about getting older is that you come to see the profound truth in even the simplest of ideas. And I'm finally beginning to understand that Time Flies.

There are too many reminders for me to ignore, especially around tax time. I'm self-employed, so I pay taxes each quarter, and on this past April 15, I thought, didn't I just pay my taxes? Was it really a few months ago, when it seems like a few minutes ago? Every time I turn around, I'm writing checks to the government, supporting all manner of astronomically expensive God-knows-whats, so that the time of my life has stretched like taffy into one continuous check written to the government.

I know I shouldn't complain about paying my taxes when there are so many Wall Street bankers who need the bonuses, Maseratis, and Manhattan brownstones that I'm buying them. And now the government is suing them for all the bad things they've done, which means that I can keep writing checks to the government to cover the costs of the litigation. This is great news, because I was afraid I would have extra money on my hands and nothing to do with it but buy dumb stuff like food, or maybe stick it in the bank, where it would help the bankers fund their defense of the litigation brought by the government on my behalf, thus maintaining my continuous stream of check-writing.

It's financial recycling.

All the money the government gets, it turns into compost.

I have the same feeling about the state, federal, and local tax bills that come in the mail more often than a Valupak, which is saying something. They break up the monotony by coming in colors, and they even have a little chart that shows how I can save money by paying today, instead of three months from now. I always pay right away, not only to save money but to avoid collisions with the other checks I'll be writing to the government. This way, I can alternate by writing checks to the state government every Monday, Wednesday, and Friday, and writing checks to the federal government every Tuesday, Thursday, and Saturday.

Of my life.

Every Sunday, I'll order more checks.

Time flies when it comes to other things, too. I have an old truck that I use sometimes, and it broke down the other day, so I had it towed to the shop, where they informed me that the last time it was inspected was January 2009.

"2009?" I was confused. "Did that come yet?"

"Sure did," answered the mechanic.

Sheesh! It doesn't even sound right. What sounds right is 1955.

The mechanic added, "Your registration expired, too."

"But I just renewed it. Did you see the sticker?"

"The last sticker on your license plate is from 2008."

"That's not possible," I said, reeling.

"I'd check, but there's no registration card in the truck."

Of course there isn't. Silly man. It's the first thing I lose. Still, I said, "Maybe the registration sticker fell off?"

"Unlikely," he said, and I knew he was right. They put Krazy Glue on those registration stickers. You could mend the space shuttle with a registration sticker.

So I had to go to the auto tag place to renew the registration, but not until I had stopped by the ATM to take out the extortionate $104 it costs, which must be paid in cash, so it can be more easily composted by the government.

And the ATM machine charged me a $3.00 fee, which will undoubtedly be sent to the bankers at their houses in the Hamptons, where they can use it to light their cigars.

So you know where this is going.

Time flies.

And so does money.

History Lesson

By Lisa

Once again, everybody's cranky about something, and I'm not.

Not that I don't get cranky, we all know that I do. For example, don't get me started on politics, taxes, or how hard it is to find jeans that fit.

But this time, everybody's cranky that a local history museum sold two thousand artifacts. Among them, a horse weathervane went for $20,000 and a cigar-store Indian sold for a million bucks.

Wow.

I'm not angry at the museum. On the contrary, I admire the museum. I wish the museum had negotiated my book contract and my last trip to the mall.

What kind of historian is financially savvy enough to sell an old weathervane for twenty grand? This would be the Donald Trump of historians. In school, I used to think history was boring, but if I had known it was worth cash money, I would have paid better attention.

And how about that cigar-store Indian?

First, did you even know a cigar-store Indian existed, outside of a cowboy movie? And second, are you allowed to say cigar-store Indian anymore, much less pay a million bucks for one? Since when are stereotypes for sale?

The only thing that bugs me is that the museum didn't try to sell me anything. My cash is as good as anybody else's. Why wasn't I offered some top quality, grade A history? And who are the new buyers?

I mean, er, historians.

We need to know their names and addresses, so we know where to go to see the history. I wonder when they'll have us over. I'm free Tuesday, but not Wednesday. How about you? I'm sure they'd be happy to show us. After all, it's our history.

Or at least it used to be.

The museum said that it sold the history to improve the museum building, which makes sense to me. What good is history without a nice building to stick it in? I think the best plan would be to sell *all* the history, then build a really gorgeous museum.

With microsuede sectionals and a plasma TV.

And the museum also said that it needed the money to provide dehumidification and air-conditioning, which is crucial to history.

Who knew?

I always thought that history got along fine without AC, but maybe not. That must be why George Washington wore a wig. His hair was a mess, in that humidity.

I can relate.

Later, after our museum gets the new air-conditioning, we can go visit anytime. The next hot day, let's all go to the museum and enjoy the cool air. We may have lost the weather-vane, but we got the weather.

Another reason I think it's okay that the history museum sold the history is that I'm jealous.

Jealous, jealous, jealous.

After all, I have history. Lots of it. And most of it isn't even as pretty as a weathervane. I really wish I could sell some of my history.

Which?

My second marriage comes immediately to mind. But nobody's dumb enough to buy that.

Except me.

Also the sixth grade. I would sell you the entire sixth grade for a song. That was not a good year in my history. I had moved to a new school and nobody liked me. And I had just gotten glasses and a bra.

I only needed one of those things.

Guess which.

iLisa

|||||||||||||||||||||||||||||||||||||||||||||||||

By Lisa

I need a smartphone, but I'm not smart enough to know which one.

First off, I'm not even sure what a smartphone is. For example, I don't know how it's different from a cellphone. I assume that a smartphone is a cellphone that does things other than make and receive phone calls, but how many things do you have to do to qualify as smart?

It's a lot to ask from an inanimate object.

Or, for that matter, from a human being.

I do only a few things, myself. Right off the top of my head, here's what I do: write things, eat things, and pet things.

I know I'm like a lot of other humans in this regard, somewhat limited in my functionality, which means that if people were cellphones, we wouldn't get into Harvard.

I own a BlackBerry, which makes and receives phone calls and emails, cruises the web, and takes pictures. It may do other things, but I don't need the other things it does.

Maybe I need a dumbphone.

Let's assume my BlackBerry is a smartphone, which makes sense. It remembers the phone numbers and email addresses of my friends, which is more than I do. And it saves all my photos in chronological order, which is also more than I do. And finally, it finds a way to cost me three hundred dollars a month, which is very smart.

In fact, it's Einstein.

But its glass has a huge crack, and it's time to replace it, especially since I got a flyer in the mail that tells me I'm eligible to upgrade my phone for less than $3 million.

Please.

Tell me I'm not the only one who's been caught in the upgrade scam, where they charge you a normal price for your phone, but if you want to upgrade within two years, you hand over your firstborn.

You can get a fairer deal from the Mafia. Organized crime takes many forms. I'm talking to you, AT&T.

The funny thing is, I'm old enough to remember all the way back in time, before portable phones and car phones, then before that to pushbutton phones and rotary phones, to the time when AT&T was the only phone company. The government said that AT&T was a monopoly that had to be broken up, supposedly to give consumers more choices, and you can judge for yourself how well that turned out, because now there are plenty of phone companies, and all of them charge you $3 million to upgrade your cellphone.

Yay!

Now, you can choose which phone company gets to raise your firstborn, which makes them a godfather. Or, er, The Godfather.

And this is when you know your government is working for you, at upgrade time.

Me, I'm thinking that we should upgrade our government.

I need to replace my smartphone, but I want to make the right choice, now that I have so many choices. So I did some research and looked at some ads, and as best I can tell, there are three basic choices in smartphones: BlackBerry, iPhone, and Android.

Sorry, I mean two choices.

Android is not a choice, for me. In any movie I've ever seen, the androids are killer robots. I won't even go to the android store.

I'm scared.

If Android, Inc. wants me to buy one of their phones, they need to change their name to one that girls like. Chocolate. Puppy. Or George Clooney.

You knew that was coming.

So I went to the Apple store, an experience you have had if you've seen the color white. And I picked up the iPhone and played with it, noticing its functions, of which there are several hundred.

Definitely, smart.

And it had a function that lets you see the person you're talking to on the phone, and vice versa. I got excited. It would be nice to see Daughter Francesca while we yapped away. And it would be fun if she could see me.

But then I thought about other people who could see me on the phone. In my bathrobe. In my glasses.

My plumber.

My electrician.

My blind date.

And then I remembered that when I'm on the phone, I sometimes write, eat, and pet things.

So I didn't buy the iPhone.

I'm too smart.

Oh, You Don't Know

IIIIIIIIIIIIIIIIIIIIIIIIIIIIIIIIIIIIIIIIIIIII

By Francesca

I look to my mom for advice about everything. I call her to ask how long to cook a chicken breast, and at what temperature to set the oven. I send her cellphone pictures of clothes I'm trying on in the dressing room. I call her when there's a mouse in my kitchen, even though she is roughly 130 miles away.

I also ask my mom for advice about men.

I just never take it.

This is not to say her advice is bad. Two marriages teach you a thing or two—at least two.

So no, her advice is far from bad. It's just Mom Advice. Nine times out of ten, I want, need, and crave Mom Advice. But modern romance is not one of those times.

So why do I keep asking?

I admit when I'm wrong, and in this case, I am. Why do I solicit my mother's opinion when I know I'll disregard it? Is this some last vestige of adolescence? Must I wean myself off my past addiction to eye-rolling and the general dismissal of all things motherly?

Oh, Mom.

It does have a nice ring to it.

And I confess, it is funny sometimes, to hear her wacky

logic. A while back, I was introduced to a cute guy at a party—I wasn't sure if I wanted to pursue him, but I didn't want to lose track of him.

"Should I friend him on Facebook?" I asked my mom.

"No, I think that's a little intrusive."

"Mom, you wanted me to get a criminal background check on that lawyer before our first date, do you remember that?"

"That was for your safety. This is different."

"*Psh,* you don't know."

But why would she know? When she was my age, people called each other on the phone. And instead of reading a list of interests online, they had to actually get to know each other, slowly. And the craziest of all: If they weren't physically in front of each other, they had to—wait for it—*imagine* what the other person looked like.

I know! Who has the time?

My mom also has impossibly high standards for dating protocol. For example, this guy I met asked me out to drinks, and I called my mom to ask her thoughts on a potential outfit, but she had other opinions:

"Drinks? You should go out to dinner."

"He didn't ask me to dinner, Mom. And anyway, drinks are fine. It's a first date."

"It's not a date. A date is a meal."

"What? There are lots of types of dates, coffee dates, lunch dates, drinks dates. C'mon."

"I don't get it. Why would you want to drink and not eat? Is he trying to get you drunk?"

"You sound crazy right now. Drinks are a perfectly normal date."

"I've never been on a 'drinks date.'"

"Never?"

"In fact, I've never been in a bar."

"Oh, forget it."

This is one of my mom's favorite myths—that she's never been in a bar. I still have a hard time believing it, but that's her story, and she's sticking to it. I know this about her, so I should've known better than to ask.

Anyway, that night, I chose my own outfit and went on my not-weird-at-all drinks date. Although my date's choice to order a bottle for the two of us was perhaps ambitious—by his third glass, his eyes were droopy, and he was repeating himself. I was bored. Didn't see him again.

But it's no big loss. I've since started seeing someone I like much better—not that that makes it any easier. My girlfriends and I have an inexhaustible tolerance for discussing the delicate, early weeks of a new relationship. Our war room strategy sessions can last upwards of an hour. So I don't know what I was thinking when I asked my civilian mom the question:

"Should I call him?"

"Do you want to see him?" my mom said.

"Well, yeah, but we texted yesterday, and he told me he might be free tonight, but we didn't make plans. Since I haven't heard from him today, I don't know if I should make other plans. I could ask him, but I don't want to seem like I'm waiting around with nothing to do, you know? Because he clearly has other things to do, otherwise he wouldn't have said the 'might' in 'might be free.'"

"I have no idea what you just said."

"Mom!"

"Do you want to see him tonight, or do you want to do something else?"

"See him."

"Then call him."

"It's not that simple. I can't just call him."

"Yes. You can."

"No, it needs finesse. I don't just want to see him; I want him to *want* to see me."

"It isn't your job to control what he wants. Your job is to figure out what you want."

And just like that, she'll say something that makes perfect sense.

So it's not that I'm wrong to ask for my mom's advice.

But every so often, I should listen.

Home, Sweet Gym

By Lisa

Everything in my home office is at my fingertips, and I'm gaining weight. I sense these things are not unrelated.

I've set up everything in my life so I don't have to move around too much, with the completely foreseeable result that now I don't move around too much. And five pounds later, it turns out it wasn't one of my better ideas.

It started last year, when I stopped working in my home office, which is upstairs. It's a converted bedroom that has a desk, TV, and bookshelves, and one side is covered with framed covers of my books, like my wall o' self-esteem.

Correction.

If I had self-esteem, I wouldn't need a wall.

But when Daughter Francesca moved out, I didn't need to stay upstairs to have quiet, and even before then I used to come downstairs and work in the kitchen, which I called my summer office.

And in my summer office, the laptop is right next to the refrigerator, but I've mentioned that before and it's not my point herein. Now I want to talk about how I've created a life that doesn't require me to move around my house, so that now I need a home gym.

Ironic, because my house used to be my gym. By this I mean when I worked in my upstairs office, I used to spend a lot of time running up and down the stairs.

My staircase was my StairMaster.

But now all I do is sit.

Also, shoved in the corner of my upstairs office was an elliptical machine. I used it when I worked up there, because I practically had to trip over it to get to my desk. But you know what they say: out of sight, out of mind.

Though I'm not sure they were talking about ellipticals.

Still, the result was the same. I was thinking that I needed a home gym when I remembered that I already had one.

Oops.

So I had no excuses.

And what happened next is that I said to myself, enough already. Get upstairs and work out on the elliptical. But I had to dress the part. I had some old shorts and a new white shirt of something called Under Armour. Actually I had bought one for Daughter Francesca, who really does work out and run, and an extra one for me, because I think about working out and running.

But when I opened up the Under Armour package, I realized that Under Armour is Spanx for jocks.

I had ordered a Medium, but this size was Postage Stamp.

I could not believe the shirt would stretch out enough for me to put it on, but I tried, and when I got it over my neck, I almost strangled myself. I managed to pop through the neck like some superannuated turtle, then I wrenched it over my shoulders and felt like I'd bound my chest, which isn't a good look for an A cup.

Still, regardless of how I looked in my Under Armour, it imparted a generally athletic vibe that made me feel good about myself.

Like a shirt o' self-esteem.

So I jumped onto the elliptical and hit the START button, exuberant until I had to plug in my weight. So I subtracted ten pounds and plugged it in.

Yes, dear reader, I lied.

To an inanimate object.

Then I started pedaling, and within thirty seconds I had to hit PAUSE button to take off my Under Armour, because I was sweating profusely.

Which must be why they call it Under Armour.

Because it makes you sweat under your armers.

Either way, in time I gave up and went down to the kitchen.

Er, I mean, my office.

The Right To Vote

||||||||||||||||||||||||||||||||||||||||||||||||||||

By Lisa

I believe it's important to vote. It's our right and privilege, as Americans. That's why I vote whenever I can, for *Dancing with the Stars, The Sing-Off,* and *American Idol.*

I vote, vote, vote.

I'm a votin' fool.

It wasn't always thus. I used to watch all those shows and never vote. I felt silly voting, even though nobody would know it. I thought there was a dividing line between people who voted and people who didn't vote.

That dividing line would be age nine.

But then, I thought about it. The person I wanted to win wasn't winning. Plus I wanted my voice to be heard, which is what makes this country great. So now, I exercise my right and privilege, and vote.

From the couch.

I text my vote, which is an idea whose time has come, if you ask me.

If we could text our votes in political elections, everybody would vote. No more worries about getting to the polls or bad weather. And texting can be made secure. For example, I can check my VISA card balance by text. And I'd rather somebody knew my vote than my VISA balance.

We should start texting votes for political elections. We'd have a hundred percent voter turnout, and our politicians would be better singers.

And better yet, you can vote more than once on TV elections. I like that. Why stop at only one vote? You can vote up to ten times, which shows you really really really meant it.

Okay, that's only three times, but you get the idea.

As a rule, I vote for my favorite TV singer only once. This is my way of saying my piece, but not trying to sway the election. I'm no control freak. I just want to make a record, even if it's only for myself.

Because my vote is secret.

You don't think I'd tell anybody that I vote for TV singers, do you?

If they ask, I'll deny it. And if they read this, I'll say I made it up.

I tell people I read at night.

I have the same attitude for the political elections, even presidential. I don't mind telling you that I didn't vote for either candidate running in this past election. I wrote in my own candidate for president, even though I knew my candidate wouldn't win. It was impossible, with only one cranky vote. But I really thought I had the best candidate, so I voted the way I wanted to, regardless of who was running. Officially.

Why get technical? I made my point, to no one.

Er, to me.

And to the hapless poll person who had to help me figure

out where to write in the name and also lent me a pen, as I didn't know I'd be doing a write-in ballot until I actually got in the booth. This is what a good planner I am, which is another reason I'm divorced twice.

Now, the only problem with voting on TV shows is that you get too invested. You really want your person to win. I guess this is like playing golf and betting on who wins each hole. I don't play golf or bet, but I'm sure it ups the ante, and the anxiety.

Either way, now that I vote, I'm nervous. What used to be entertainment has become a cause. For example, right now, I'm waiting for *The Sing-Off* finale to come on TV, and I couldn't decide who was the best *a cappella* group, so last week, I voted for the two best groups. And I voted once for each.

Again, not trying to sway, just trying to represent.

Myself.

I'm *a cappella,* after all. I can relate.

But now I'm worried that my candidates may not win, even though they're the most deserving. I can tell they're not the judges' favorites, though they should be.

I hate it when voting gets political, don't you?

The Einstein Workout

||||||||||||||||||||||||||||||||||||||||||||

By Lisa

Einstein discovered that time is relative, and I bet I know where he was when he figured that one out.

On an elliptical machine.

Five minutes never seemed so long as when I'm on the elliptical, which I started doing again because it's too snowy to walk the dogs. The dogs don't do the elliptical. They watch me, and laugh.

Ruby holds the stopwatch.

There's nothing I can do to make time go faster on the elliptical. I have the TV on while I shuffle my feet and pump my arms, but my eyes keep straying to the glowing digital numerals of the clock on the console. I start watching the time around two minutes in, and as the numbers change from 2:36 to 2:37, it feels as if a second lasts twenty minutes. Sometimes I play a game with myself, where I cover the clock with a towel, but that drives me nuts, because I want to know how much torture I have left.

Er, I mean how much time I have left.

When I remove the towel, the time is always the same: More than I thought. Way more.

The other day I tapped the lighted clock with my finger, just to make sure it was working. It worked fine.

I didn't.

It reminded me of the time I was giving a speech and nobody was laughing. I would've bet that the microphone was off, but it wasn't.

I was.

Or another time, when I was trying to establish myself as a writer and I thought that the way to do that was to write a screenplay. So I did, and I sent it to a hundred agents in LA. I'm not joking or exaggerating, for once. I sent it to a hundred agents. How many replies did I get?

None.

I felt sure something was wrong with my mailbox, my zip code, the postal service, or the universe in general. But no, I was just failing.

Same thing with the elliptical.

Failing, failing, failing.

I'm good at failing. I take failure well. You can, too. Just practice.

I try to do thirty minutes on the elliptical, but I'm theorizing that the time you spend working out is like dog years. If you do it for half an hour, it will be the same as seven years.

Relatively speaking.

On the other hand, the new year just came and went, and I feel as if 2010 flew by. In fact, if you had asked me which was longer, a half an hour on an elliptical or the whole of 2010, you know which I'd pick.

Right.

Birthdays work this way, too. For example, I suppose that in some technical sense, I'm 55 years old. But it seems like I'm 25, in my mind.

Wait. I just got an idea.

I'm going to live my whole entire life on the elliptical. Then it will seem like I've lived seven lifetimes.

What a concept!

And I would never embarrass myself, as in did the other night when I was out to dinner with Daughter Francesca, Best Friend Franca, and her daughter Jessica. Franca and I were in the same law school class, and we were talking about our upcoming class reunion. I couldn't remember which one it was, so I said:

"It's our twentieth, right?".

And Franca said, "No, it's our twenty-fifth, isn't it?"

Obviously neither of us was good at math, which is why we went to law school, but Francesca and Jessica started smiling.

Francesca said, "You graduated from law school in 1981, so it's your thirtieth reunion."

Franca and I looked at each other, nonplussed. "Is that possible?" she asked.

"Of course not," I answered, and we both reached for our wine.

The fastest time of all, of course, is how long it takes for your kid to grow up. Francesca is about to turn twenty-five, and this is obviously mathematically impossible.

Because then we would be the same age.

Also she was only ten years old yesterday, and the day before that, she was a toddler, and a split second before that, a baby.

I mean, she should still be nursing.

I let down just thinking about that, but don't tell her.

I don't know how all this happened, with the time flying and the children growing, and the elliptical being so damn slow.

That Einstein, he really was a genius.

But I bet he had a trainer.

Remembering Joy

||||||||||||||||||||||||||||||||||||||||||||||||||

By Francesca

My beloved horse, Joy, recently passed away. A beautiful gray Thoroughbred mare, she was the first horse I owned and the first one I lost. I was in the city when it happened, I felt far away from anyone who could really understand. It was hard for even me to understand. It felt so different from losing a dog or a cat, not better or worse, but different.

Every pet has a unique personality, my cat is different from my dog, my dog Pip is different from my mom's dog Tony. But my relationship to each of them is the same: just love. I ask nothing of Pip except to be vaguely cooperative and accept my near-constant affection.

I asked my horse to carry me on her back. We were partners. Joy and I worked together, trained together, and learned from each other. You have to respect a horse—after all, they are large, powerful animals and they can be dangerous, intentionally or inadvertently. And yet, they mostly take care of us.

Joy certainly did.

Which is not to say she was a saint. Joy could be a difficult horse, but she was never a mean one. She was a challenge and a babysitter at the same time. Everything about riding her was outside of my comfort zone but not outside of my ability. It's in that space between where growth happens, and grow I did.

Joy raised me.

When we met, we were almost the same age, she was eleven and I was twelve. I remember when the horse dealer, a weathered ex-jockey, Rumpelstiltskin in cowboy boots, delivered her. He unceremoniously yanked on her snowy white tail to pull her out of the trailer, and out she came, her swan neck held sky high, her big brown eyes rimmed in white.

We both looked wide-eyed at each other, spooked. I was afraid because I had lived too little, Joy was afraid because she had lived too much. The mare had been bought and sold several times, loved and unloved by then; she came to us neglected and underweight. She was a nervous horse and I was a timid rider, not usually an ideal combination.

But we were.

Joy was the antidote to all my preteen insecurities, because she mirrored them. If I was afraid, she was afraid. If I second-guessed myself, she second-guessed me. If I became frustrated, she became ornery.

Crossing water was one of our major challenges. The smallest creek on a trail ride was terrifying to Joy. As soon as the water touched her hoof, she'd fly back and upwards. If she sensed we were heading near the creek, or if she sensed my own anxious anticipation, she'd crow-hop, threatening to rear.

When I felt Joy's back tense, my instinct was to tighten up, curl into a ball, anything to steady her and my pounding heart. But that never got me over the stream. A few times, it almost landed me on the ground.

Joy needed me to lead by example. I learned that I had to

relax, or at least pretend to relax, and push forward. A horse can't throw you if you keep moving forward.

And it has worked for every obstacle in my life since. Through breakups, disappointments, down days, and down months, I think of the riding command: *leg on.*

Nothing can throw you if you keep moving forward.

But even as I move forward through this loss, I will never forget the wonderful friend and teacher I had in Joy. I didn't get to be with her when she passed, but more than getting to say goodbye, I wish I had had the chance to thank her for all her many lessons:

That a strong hand can still be a gentle one. That you must be patient, with others and with yourself. Self-doubt is natural but not insurmountable. You may step into water not knowing

Angels come in many forms.

how deep it is. You may face a jump higher than before. And sometimes, as hard as it is, you need to point yourself at that obstacle and go forward. Courage is a choice.

If you live outside of your comfort zone, you might have the ride of your life.

Leg on.

911

|||||||||||||||||||||||||||||||||||||||||||||||||||||

By Lisa

Everybody reacts differently in emergencies. Some people panic and run around like crazy. Other people remain cool and spring immediately into action.

And then there's me.

I do neither. I go into emergency denial.

Here's what happened, most recently.

Daughter Francesca was home, and we were both in the family room, I was working on my laptop, and she was watching *Castle* on TV. All the dogs were with us, dozing on the couch, except for Little Tony.

Odd.

Because he spends every night standing at the window and barking at the dark.

Little Tony does not go gently into that good night.

I know how he thinks. He thinks there are dragons and sea monsters and constellations come to life in the nighttime, and he barks to keep them at bay. Never mind that he weighs ten pounds, so at his most menacing, he looks like a really angry black bean.

Francesca, sitting opposite me, asks, "How can you stand that barking?"

I'm on the laptop not five feet from Little Tony, but I've learned to tune him out. "What barking?" I ask her.

In time the barking stops, but I don't notice that either, until Francesca remarks, "Where's Little Tony?"

And I start to wonder. Little Tony is nowhere in sight. I set the laptop aside and go in search, and I find him in the kitchen, where he looks up at me and swallows hard.

Gulp, he goes.

Hmm. And next to him on the floor is one of my knee socks. You don't have to be Castle to figure out what happened. I pick up the leftover sock and can't tell by looking how much he ate, so I try it on. The entire foot is gone.

"Call the emergency vet," Francesca says, but I'm not so sure.

"It's not an emergency. Let's see if he passes it tomorrow."

"I don't think so, Mom. We should call."

"Nah." I wave her off. "They'll just say to bring him in. It can wait. He'll be fine."

"Let's play it safe, and call. Please?"

So I call and they say bring him in, and we do, waiting in the reception area an hour until they come out with him and tell us that they saved his life.

I feel terrible. "Really?"

"Yes," the vet nods. "The sock was thin and stretchy, so he wouldn't have passed it. Good thing you called."

My face goes red.

Francesca looks over.

Little Tony burps.

Then the very next day, I'm on my laptop, and it's windy outside. I hear a weird noise outside, so I look out the window and notice that a huge evergreen in my yard has fallen over onto the roof of my garage.

I blink and blink. It takes me moments to process.

This could definitely be an emergency.

The tree trunk is horizontal, which is distinctly out of order.

Still, it doesn't look as if the garage roof is damaged, and amazingly, there are no people, dogs, cats, or cars in harm's way. Everything's normal except that the big tree is parallel to the driveway. But Francesca isn't there to tell me I should call somebody, and I'm not sure whom to call. Now that I've learned from last night that I go into emergency denial, I won't make that mistake again.

Still, is it an emergency or not?

So I get on the phone and call my insurance company, which tells me that my deductible is $2500.

I eye the tree and figure it will cost a grand to clear it away.

And then I learned how to define an emergency.

Anything over your deductible.

If a Tree Falls in a Driveway...

|||||||||||||||||||||||||||||||||||||||||||||||||||||||

By Lisa

So a tree landed on my garage, but didn't damage anything. That would be the good, and the bad, news.

It got me looking at the trees around my house, and there are plenty of them. More good and bad news.

I don't know what type of trees they are, because it never mattered to me. I operate on the principle that there's only so much information my tiny little brain can hold, and it's already stuffed with things I need to know for work, plus essentials like the words to most Rolling Stones songs and the Empire Flooring jingle.

So I never learned the names of the trees I own. I'd be happy to name them Mick and Keith, and let it go at that.

But I do love the way they look, especially in fall, when they turn bright yellow and gorgeous orange, or in summer, when their rich green shades the lawn. Bottom line, we can all agree, trees are good.

Usually.

But then I started eyeing the trees, close up, and with the leaves fallen, I could see a lot of old branches, thick, dark, and ending in a point. I'm no expert, but some looked dead. I started to wonder when they might fall, like daggers from heaven.

Call this an exaggeration, but recall that I was raised by Mother Mary, who taught me that even the most mundane items can kill you. For example, knives loaded into the dishwasher will stab you. Blowdryers will electrocute you. Toasters have murder on their minds.

So I started to see the trees not as examples of natural beauty, but as lethal weapons.

And they could fall at any second, on me, the dogs, or the cats. And some of my trees hang over my street, and I'd hate to think they could fall on a passing car or person. I couldn't live with myself if that happened.

I have enough guilt already.

And made me worry about something worse.

Namely, lawyers.

So I called a tree service guy, who came over and started pointing. He knew the names of all the trees. Hemlock. Sugar maple. Red oak. Mulberry. Tulip poplar.

What lovely words.

Then he started in with the numbers—

$450, $340, $540. Not so lovely.

And then sent me a two-page estimate.

What was it that Joyce Kilmer wrote? I think that I shall never see, a poem lovely as a tree . . . service estimate?

It turns out that I have lots of trees that need servicing. Dead branches have to be trimmed, stumps ground down and hauled away. We're talking days of work.

For trees?

I expect to pay for home improvement, but I never factored in tree improvement. It reminded me of the time I had to call an excavator to build a swale in my backyard, and if

It made a sound.

you don't know what a swale is, it's like a berm, only more expensive.

No, I don't know what a berm is either. That's why it costs extra. Things add up when you start with dirt improvement.

And some of the tree improvement sounded downright exotic. For example, the tree guy told me that it was a spruce tree that fell on the garage, and it would cost $380 to reduce the top leaders.

I didn't know what a top leader was, but it sounded redundant. Nobody follows a bottom leader.

Can you imagine, a bottom leader running for president? No, we can't! Give up and go home!

Hmm.

And it would cost $90 for a fir tree that needed cable. I didn't know trees had cable. Do they have DVRs, too?

And some of it was scary. The estimate read that my sugar maple had to be pruned "to prevent main trunk failure."

That can't be good, can it?

Plus I think it already happened.

To my waist.

As Seen On TV

|||||||||||||||||||||||||||||||||||||||||||||||||||

By Lisa

I have some good news that may interest our regular readers.

And by the way, God bless you, every one.

As you may know, these stories have been collected into two previous books, entitled *Why My Third Husband Will Be a Dog* and *My Nest Isn't Empty, It Just Has More Closet Space*.

The big news is that the books have been optioned to produce a half-hour comedy series, for TV.

Yes, that's right. Mother Mary could be coming to a TV near you.

Run screaming.

Let me explain what this means, if you're unfamiliar with legal terms like "option" and "run screaming."

An option means that somebody has the right to make a TV show from the books. It doesn't mean that they necessarily will. So we can still expect that nothing will happen, which is the way it usually goes, at least for me. Not to brag, but my books have been optioned before.

I'm no Option Virgin.

But they've never made it to any screen.

So I'm a Success Virgin.

Still, this time, if it does happen, you know whom I'd suggest to play me.

Angelina Jolie.

Done deal, right? I'm sure she'd say yes. And while she's out filming the show, I could take care of Brad Pitt.

Uh, I mean, the kids.

And whom should we cast as Daughter Francesca? I say nobody is sweet or smart enough, but she thinks I'm biased. Guilty as charged.

And who should play Mother Mary?

I'd say the Tasmanian Devil, but his hands are too little to hold a backscratcher.

My second choice would be Yosemite Sam, but he's usually in too good a mood. Though he has two guns, which makes him almost as lethal as Mother Mary.

Send in your casting suggestions. Think out of the box. Be not afraid. I won't tell her where you live.

I haven't even gotten to the point where I visualize which stories they would use for which episode. All of them show me in such a flattering light. There's the Story of My Gray Chin Hair. The Tale of My Braless ER Visit. The Saga of My Crusty Feet and Amazing Disappearing Little Toe.

Stay tuned for more celibacy.

And if you're wondering, I won't be writing the TV series. I don't want to leave the house, much less go to LA. I know my fleece-pants-and-clogs ensemble wouldn't go over on Rodeo Drive.

It ain't my first rodeo.

Heh heh.

I broke the news about the TV series on book tour, and

seriously folks, that's when I realized how it cool it would be if it did become a TV series. Because I felt honored to meet everyone who read the books over the past few years. They started as the stories of my life and grew organically to encompass stories from the lives of Francesca, Mother Mary, Best Friend Franca, and assistant Laura. And by some amazing alchemy conjured by reader and writer, it became stories of the lives of ordinary women.

In other words, all of us.

I know this is true because of all the people I met at the signings, more and more of them mothers, daughters, and grandmothers, who see themselves in our relationship, because they feel the same way about each other. It turns out there are many other Mother Marys in the world.

And more than enough gray chin hairs.

And I'm not the only Spanx-hater.

And joking aside, I'm so happy to have some positive images of the mother-daughter relationship out there, and if it makes it onto TV, all the better.

For this reason, the TV series won't use my real name for the main character, or for Mother Mary or Francesca.

It really isn't about us, it's about you.

So thanks for reading, and for your loyalty.

And stay tuned.

In Which We Get A Woman President

||||||||||||||||||||||||||||||||||||||||||||||||||

By Lisa

I'm having a change of life, but I'm not sure it's the one you're thinking of:

I'm incorporating.

Yes, I'm becoming a corporation, and I'm not even on flax-seed.

Long story short, after writing almost twenty books in about twenty years, it's time for me to become a company. It was a lawyer who told me this, and the reason was to protect me from other lawyers.

Which sounds like Ted Bundy warning you to stay away from Jeffrey Dahmer.

The lawyer convinced me that incorporating was a good idea by saying the words *lawsuit* and *exposure,* which scared me. I never want to be exposed. If you had my cellulite, you'd understand.

And I have to admit, the idea of incorporating appealed to my ego. After all, if I became a corporation, you know who would be the president.

Ruby The Crazy Corgi.

No, me.

Call me President Me.

But don't tell Ruby. She scares me more than *exposure*. She's the dog that ate the top of my finger, biting the hand that feeds her, literally.

Anyway, to stay on point, it also seemed like I'd be taking a step up, going from being self-employed to becoming my own company. I felt suddenly more legitimate, like a couple who had been living together but decided to get married. Except I was marrying myself.

This time, I'm sure it'll work!

My third husband won't be a dog or a big TV, it'll be me. After all, we never fight, we always agree, and we have the same religion, which is worshipping chocolate cake.

So during the big meeting to discuss the particulars, the first question the lawyers asked me was, "What do you want to call your corporation?"

"I don't know," I answered. During any big meeting, I'm always the one not knowing. "What should I call my corporation?"

"Just pick a name you like," they answered, so I told them: "Microsoft."

They didn't think it was funny. Or maybe they hear it 300 times a day. They asked, "How about Lisa Scottoline, LLC?"

It had a familiar ring, but it wasn't much fun. I thought about it. I always notice the company names at the end of TV shows and movies, and a lot of them are fun. I needed to think of a fun corporate name. After all, I envisioned myself as a fun company president, like the corporate version of the Cool Mom.

Also I realized that was failing the first test of President Me, in asking them what to name the company instead of making an Executive Decision, all by my presidential self. So I told them I'd think about it, which meant I went home and asked Daughter Francesca.

She said, "How about Smart Blonde?"

I loved it immediately, and I decided to become Smart Blonde, LLC. Instead of Dumb Blonde, get it? Changing the world, one stereotype at a time.

Very presidential.

I'm the change candidate.

By the way, don't ask me what LLC means. I know that LL Cool J means Ladies Love Cool J. So maybe LLC means Ladies Love C something.

I know.

Ladies Love Chocolate Cake!

I should have named my corporation LLC, LLC, then only those of us in the know would get it. Everybody else would think I was drunk.

Back to the story. After I had the corporate name, the lawyers said they'd draw up the papers, but oddly, I found myself lying awake at night, anxious about my life change. I didn't know if I was ready to be President. I feel more comfy being Class Clown.

And I'd never had a woman president, much less been one.

Then I realized.

Like many women, I run a household. All moms have.

We're all presidents of our homes. We plan and run everybody's schedules, we coordinate the pick-ups and the deliveries.

We authorize certain expenditures and disallow others. We make sure there's heat, clean clothes, packed lunches. We make sure there's something other than pizza for dinner.

So it's not as if we've never had a woman president.

In fact, we always have.

She's us.

Now all we need is a raise.

The Hardest Job in the World

|||||||||||||||||||||||||||||||||||||||||||||||||

By Francesca

I've always known what it's like to have a great mother, but I had no idea what it's like to *be* a great mother. Having one dog can't really approximate what it's like to be a mom.

That takes at least three dogs.

My mother was recently traveling on tour with her latest book, and it was a grueling schedule; a different city every other day, high-energy signings, meetings with booksellers, and greasy airport food. She loves it, but it's a tough job.

Still, it ain't nothin' compared with being a stay-at-home-mom.

I should know, I was taking care of our three dogs while she was away.

In addition to my own dog, Pip, I had *two* of my mother's dogs, Little Tony, and the new baby, six-month-old Peach. I'm happy to help my mom whenever I can, so I told her it wouldn't be a problem. But it was much harder than I anticipated. It was like caring for human children.

Maybe it was the diapers.

But I'm getting ahead of myself.

I grew up as an only child, but I'd heard the clichés about sibling dynamics—the oldest golden child, the attention-loving baby, the overlooked middle child. I never knew they were true:

Peach is tiny, adorable, and accident-prone. I carried her wherever I went and otherwise kept her on my lap so I could make sure she didn't get into stuff, put anything in her mouth, or pee on the floor.

Pip, my oldest, is the best behaved and my first love, so he was on his own with occasional praise for being a very good boy.

As for Little Tony, the middle child, I forgot he existed until he did something bad.

They have therapists for dogs, right?

While I struggled to divide my time and love equally, I nearly missed a major milestone in my little girl's life—Peach's first period.

I know, I couldn't believe it either. But call it a mother's intuition, or call it a red spot on my couch, I just knew.

But what do you do when a dog becomes a woman?

Are you there, God? It's me, Francesca, and I have this dog . . .

The first problem is that Peach is tiny. The puppy weighs less than ten pounds, so I had to try a slew of pet stores to find doggie diapers small enough to fit.

Not that she allowed them to stay on her body. Peach tried to pull, squirm, and chew herself free from her diaper.

Babies are so fussy.

During the brief moments when Peach tired and left the diaper alone, Tony bothered it for her.

Mother's little helper.

On top of it all, I got sick as a dog, no pun. The unpredictable spring weather left me with an awful head cold. But as every parent knows, moms can't get sick. Rather, if they do, it doesn't count.

I needed Sudafed but I didn't want to leave the little ones at home, so I found myself standing in the pharmacy line, holding the puppy on my hip, with the two others wrapped around my legs.

People were staring, but I didn't care. All I could think about was how much time I had before Tony needed to go to the bathroom, how many diapers we had left at home, and whether Pip ate a wad of gum that I could've sworn was on the floor a minute ago.

I had crossed a threshold. The dogs had become my priority.

Although dogs, even three of them, aren't the same as children, the priority shift is the same as every mother's. My mom changed her career, her entire life, to stay home with me. She has put me first in every decision she's ever made. And as a result, she is the first person I turn to in every one of mine.

I want to thank the mothers who do the difficult, tiring, messy, comical, selfless work of putting us first. You're number one to us.

Until we have kids of our own.

Just like you taught us.

This Land Is My Land

||||||||||||||||||||||||||||||||||||||||||||||||||||

By Lisa

I'm still on book tour, which means that by the time you read this, I'll be eating my 307th airport burrito.

That's not the bad news.

I'm in love with airport food. I'm on a different plane every day, sometimes two, so I usually eat in the airport, and my book tour is an excuse to have Auntie Annie's pretzels, TCBY vanilla fro-yo with jimmies, and Sbarro pepperoni pizza. It's America on 5000 Carbs a Day, only literary.

By Day Eight, I thought I should try to eat healthy, so I settled for an apple with a barcode sticker. You haven't lived until you've eaten fruit you can scan. I tried to take off the sticker, but it was affixed with Krazy Glue, because God forbid it falls off and some unfortunate cashier has to hit a key. Or worse, God forbid there's no sticker but the cashier has to memorize the price of the apple, which is like twenty dollars.

In the end, I eat around the sticker, after I take the apple to the women's restroom in Terminal B, where washing it only makes it dirtier.

Airport food is just one part of the fun of travel.

I find myself standing behind a very old man in line at airport security, and he has never flown before, so he has never done the drill of shoes off, jacket in bin, spare change in plastic bowl.

He turns to me and says: "A thousand bucks for a ticket and I gotta take my sneakers off. Sheesh!"

"I know, right?" I say, which is an all-purpose response that indicates agreement, commiseration, or affability in general.

Still, he asks, "Why I gotta do that?"

I blink. "It's because of the terrorists."

"What terrorists?" he asks, raising a gray eyebrow.

Obviously, I'm in line behind Rip Van Winkle, but I take pity on him. I could be him when I get older, under the testy stares of the TSA types and the undisguised grousing of the travelers behind us. He keeps going through the metal detector, but it beeps every time, sending him back to the line.

He turns bewildered to me, his hooded eyes shining unhappily. "What do I do?"

"Let me help." So I ease him out of his shoes, then his jacket, then his clunky ancient watch. Still the metal detector beeps, and he comes back. Like a child, he lifts up his shirt, revealing a fake-silver belt buckle the size of Texas.

Which is where I draw the line.

I tell him, "You have to take off your own belt, sir."

He looks disappointed, but I stand firm. I don't take off a man's belt unless he buys me an airport enchilada.

Call me old-fashioned.

But my favorite part of travel is the gift shop. If you've ever wondered who's the idiot that buys all that dumb junk, she would be me.

Bottom line is that I love airport gift shops. There're the only places in the country that are still regional. Think about it.

If you go out for a drive, everywhere you look, you'll pass a Chili's, a Gap, and a McDonald's, so that the whole nation looks the same, one state to the next.

Real America awaits you in the airport gift shop.

There you can find T-shirts from the hometown baseball/ basketball/hockey team, or all-cotton T-shirts bearing the city's name, with sexual innuendos in local motifs. For example, the New York T-shirts have apples over the breasts, the Detroit T-shirts have tires over the breasts, and the L.A. shirts have Hollywood sunglasses over the breasts.

See? Regional.

Plus the gift shops sell other local items. The gift shop in the Houston airport sells bottles of five-alarm barbecue sauce, the gift shop in the Chicago airport sells the four-pack of brat-wurst, the gift shop in Dallas sells the straw cowgirl hat, and the gift shop in the Phoenix airport sells the plant-it-yourself cactus kit. I buy the cactus kit for Daughter Francesca, who's delighted. She pours the fake-orange sand into its adobe-hued pot and plants the miniature bulb of prickly cactus. The cactus kit even comes with a tiny wooden sign that reads ARIZONA, in burnt brown letters like an Old-West brand.

"You don't have to use the sign," I tell her.

"But I like the sign." Francesca smiles. "The sign is the best part."

Secretly, I agree.

And I'm proud.

What a kid.

And what a country.

The Four Seasons

||||||||||||||||||||||||||||||||||||||||||||||||||||||

By Lisa

I've joked about hot flashes and gray chin hairs, but I've never really talked about aging, straight-up.

Though I've been thinking about it, like most women, and I have opinions. Like most women.

God bless us.

So here's what I think.

We begin not with winter, but with spring.

I walked the dogs today and saw my first crocus. Soon, lawns will be growing grass, tender and weak enough to be flattened by the cat's paw. Trees will be budding with tiny specks of green, their color oddly bright, like Andes mint wrappers. Rosebushes, tight-fisted, will withhold their flowers until later, unfurling only after water, sunshine, and time give them life.

Everybody loves spring. You know why?

It's young.

And people say they love the seasons.

Really? Do they love winter? I don't mean winter when it's easy to love. I don't mean first-snow winter, with its homey blanket of confectioner's sugar. Or snow-globe winter, with its oversized flakes filling the air, swirling around on picturesque gusts.

I'm talking freezing, wet, snowblower winter, with endless storms, plowing, and salting. Snow that clumps ugly on the shady side of the house. Snow days until even the kids want to go back to school. Until nobody wants to bake another chocolate chip cookie. At some point, every winter becomes the winter of our discontent.

Nasolabial-fold winter, if you follow.

What got me thinking about this was the umpteenth skin product that advertised itself as "age-defying." They want to sell us creams, lotions, and magic potions to "defy" our age. They tell us that the way to be beautiful is to "erase our fine lines and wrinkles" and "Defy Father Time!"

Huh?

Who started the war?

Who said we have to fight?

Why do we have to take up arms against our flabby arms?

What's up with all the age-defying handbooks and age-defying secrets?

And it's not only the cosmetic companies. Certain foods are touted as "anti-aging," drafting even avocados and broccoli into the war on aging.

But vegetables aren't anti-aging. They're not anti-anything.

And finally, neither am I.

Here's my credo in life: Fight only the battles that matter, and after that, only the ones you can win.

And defying your age is a losing battle.

In other words:

Peace.

Acceptance. Tolerance. Appreciation. If you love the spring, you have to love the winter, and it's all part of the same whole, no matter what Revlon says.

We can't be young women forever.

We can't even look like young women forever.

And we have to stop fighting.

Give peace a chance.

Now, don't get all literal on me. To be clear, I have no problem with anybody who Botoxes and fills. To each her own. I fake my hair color and wear contacts. But ultimately, there's a difference between wanting to look your best and denying who you are.

And that's a question that each of us answers for herself. And answers only to herself.

I'm talking about the woman in the mirror.

I know that aging isn't always easy to accept. It takes strength of character to look age in the face, to see all of its wrinkles and not-so-fine lines. It takes decades to build the kind of fortitude you need to get older.

Aging is not for the young.

If you follow.

For example, I used to eat everything and never gained weight. Now I eat nothing and gain weight. I gain weight when I even look at food. Inhaling Cinnabons puts on five pounds.

But now, I don't worry so much about how I look. Because the truth is, fewer people are looking.

And you can see that as bad news, or good. For me, I'll choose the good. It's freeing. I worry less, and women are so good at worrying that we do it second nature, not realizing what a heavy burden it is until we set it down.

And now that I'm not so worried about how I look, I do more things in the time I have, and at the end of my life, I'd rather have done more, looking worse, than done less, looking better.

In fact, I want my tombstone to read: SHE DID A TON. AND SHE DIDN'T BOTHER TO CHANGE OUT OF HER SWEATS.

Every woman writes her own story, and it's the story of her own life.

And everything that happens to us, like the birth of a child or a grandchild, is a sentence.

A line, if you will.

And our job, as the author of our life story, is to live so that each one of our lines is fine. Beautiful, even.

So throw away your eraser.

And write well.

Better yet, write beautifully.

The Best Friends Part

||||||||||||||||||||||||||||||||||||||||||||||||||

By Lisa

A great thing about having a daughter is that she can introduce you to aspects of the "youth culture," like hip and cool books, TV, and music. And you can teach her ancient history, like Steely Dan, Nancy Drew, and Ozzie & Harriet.

A band from the fifties, right?

For example, Daughter Francesca has introduced me to a lot of new music, like Rufus Wainright, who's so hip he wrote a song entitled, "My Phone Is on Vibrate for You."

It's a love song. To a person, not a BlackBerry.

It's not the kind of song that my generation could have had, since in those days, our phones had wires, and we didn't have anything that vibrated. At least not that I remember. I myself haven't vibrated in some time, but I'm straying from my point.

It's cool to share stuff you love with your daughter, and sometimes you love the same thing, which is striking generational gold. Of course, this isn't confined to mothers and daughters. I remember playing the Beach Boys' album *Pet Sounds* for my father, and he loved it. In return, he played a Nina Simone record for me.

You may have to look up these arcane references, like "album" and "record."

Lisa and Francesca, best friends

There are many TV shows, movies, and books that Francesca and I both love, but there is nothing we love quite as much as one TV show in particular. I'm talking, of course, about *Sex and the City*.

OMG!!!!!

We became fangirls at the very mention of the title, and we love every episode, which we have memorized. We love the movies, too, and we hope they make more sequels, so we can have more *Sex and the City* to see, talk about, cry and laugh over. We love the actresses who play the girls, especially Sarah Jessica Parker as Carrie and Cynthia Nixon as Miranda, and we love the friendship between the girls, Carrie, Miranda, Charlotte, and Samantha.

So it's easy to understand why, when I heard that Cynthia

Nixon occasionally records audiobooks, I asked my publisher if we could get her to record the audiobook of my next novel, entitled *Save Me*. The planets aligned, and so it came to pass that Francesca and I were in a recording studio in New York, and sitting on the other side of the room, behind the glass like some rare and beautiful jewel, was Cynthia Nixon.

Cue angels.

We listened, rapt, as she performed my novel, and she made even my writing sound good.

Now *that's* talent!

Francesca and I had recorded the audiobooks for these books, and how difficult it was, and all I had to do was be me. It took my total concentration and three days to read every word of a book aloud, not counting the effort to downplay my Philadelphia accent.

Yo!

But the recording of a novel is something different altogether. *Save Me* has an array of characters, female and male, and its co-star is an eight-year-old girl. With a sore throat.

No joke.

And Cynthia Nixon had to do all of these voices, including the sore throat, acting out not only everybody in the novel, but characterizing them more deeply, using only the nuances of voice, inflection, and intonation. She was amazing, and more than that, I was reminded of how great an audiobook is, probably the closest we get, in our technological age, to being told a story around a fire.

During the lunch break, we got to eat with Cynthia, the sound engineer from the studio, and Laura Wilson, the audio genius from my publisher. The whole time, Cynthia was a down-to-earth, incredibly nice person, and she didn't act like the goddess she is or could be. Francesca was adorable and charming, and I prayed there was no food in my teeth.

After lunch, we went back to the recording studio, listened to Cynthia work her magic, then left before we embarrassed ourselves any further. We talked all the way home, when our conversation morphed from Miranda to the mother in the novel, then to motherhood in general, and finally, to mothers and daughters.

It was one of our best talks ever.

Which is, after all, the purpose of the arts. Books, music, movies, opera, plays, paintings, they're all of a piece. To me, their highest and best purpose is to bring people closer, to connect them one to the other.

Even people who were already close, like Francesca and me.

Peace and love *(Photograph by April Narby)*

We're best friends, after all.

And our relationship is made every day, in fights over green jackets, as well as in much sweeter moments like the ones we shared that afternoon, when we were two girlfriends, adoring our favorite girlfriend. Francesca and I make the good and the bad moments, all the time, every day, and it forms the very stuff of our bond.

I know there are lots of mothers and daughters in the world who are also best friends, and we're all of us very lucky in each other.

And for those of you who aren't there yet, may I just say that that can always be changed?

Fixed, in a New York minute.

Because when Francesca and I fuss, I can feel the power I have as her mother. We, all of us moms, have that power. So if you're a mother fussing with your daughter right now, or even for the past year or years, you can change that. Don't wait for her to come around.

Go first.

You're the mother, right? And the alleged adult.

So say you're sorry. Set it right. Do what it takes.

It's not hard to make that first step when you remember how much you love her. How lucky you are to have her. Keep in mind, always, that you love her, and she loves you.

Love really is the answer.

And no one loves better, stronger, or harder than a mother.

So be her best friend.

And you'll get a best friend.

For life.

Acknowledgments

||||||||||||||||||||||||||||||||||||||||||||||

By Lisa and Francesca

We're both big fans of thanks and love, so thank you so much and love to everyone at St. Martin's Press for supporting this book and its predecessors. First and foremost, thanks to Coach Jen Enderlin, our terrific editor, as well as to the brilliant John Sargent, Sally Richardson, Matthew Shear, George Witte, Matt Baldacci, Brian Keller, Jeff Capshew, Steve Cohen, Alison Lazarus, Steve Kleckner, Ken Holland, Merrill Bergenfeld, John Edwards, Martin Quinn, Tom Siino, Christine Jaeger, Rob Renzler, Talia Sherer, Jaime Ariza, Astra Berzinskas, Michael Storrings, John Murphy, Dori Weintraub, John Karle, Monica Katz, Nancy Trypuc, Kim Ludlum, Anne Marie Tallberg, Joe Goldschein, and Sara Goodman. We appreciate so much your enthusiasm for these books, and we thank you for everything.

Thanks so much and love to Mary Beth Roche, Laura Wilson, Anne Gardner, and the other great people at St. Martin's audiobook division. Stories are meant to be told, not read, which is why we love audiobooks. And thanks for giving us the chance to record our own audiobooks, for which we even won two "Earphones" Awards, given by the prestigious *Audio-File Magazine*. We're two for two, and that doesn't happen without great direction and production. Yay, team!

Thanks and love to our amazing agents, Molly Friedrich, Paul Cirone, and Lucy Carson of the Friedrich Agency. They're the smartest, funniest, and most loyal bunch you'll ever meet. God bless them for their hard work and great hearts.

Thanks to *The Philadelphia Inquirer,* which publishes our "Chick Wit" column every Sunday, and to our editor, the wonderful Sandy Clark.

One of the biggest hearts in creation belongs to Laura Leonard, and her friendship sustains us. We love you, Laura, and thank you for helping us every day, in every way, and with this book. Laura keeps us straight on every line, and thanks so much for that. Plus you're a great mom, and you raised us both.

Love to our girlfriends, a conspiracy of moms and daughters, among them Nan Daley and Nora and Jolie Demchur, Paula Menghetti and Bev, Tori, and Alex, Franca Palumbo and Jessica Limbacher, and of course, Molly Friedrich and Julia, Lucy, and Pi-qui Carson. We've all watched each other grow up, and we're blessed in that, and so much else.

Family is the heart of this book, because family is the heart of everything. Thanks and all our love to Mother Mary and Brother Frank, who deserves a book unto himself. We still miss every day the late Frank Scottoline, but he is with us always.

Finally, we knew we were lucky before we wrote this book, but we're most lucky in our readers, who have shared our stories and even told us some of their own, in email and on tour. You're family now, too.

We're stuck with each other, from now on. And for that, we extend our sincerest thanks to each of you, and our love.

This is a hug.